JOHN GOHORRY
BOLD HEART

JOHN GOHORRY
BOLD HEART

*Poems from Ten Books
& Essays by Divers Hands*

EDITED BY STUART HENSON

All rights reserved. No part of this work covered by the copyright herein may be reproduced or used in any means – graphic, electronic, or mechanical, including copying, recording, taping, or information storage and retrieval systems – without written permission of the publisher.

Printed by imprintdigital
Upton Pyne, Exeter
www.digital.imprint.co.uk

Typesetting and cover design by The Book Typesetters
us@thebooktypesetters.com
07422 598 168
www.thebooktypesetters.com

Published by Shoestring Press
19 Devonshire Avenue, Beeston, Nottingham, NG9 1BS
(0115) 925 1827
www.shoestringpress.co.uk

First published 2022
© Copyright: John Gohorry
© Essays copyright individual contributors
© Cover photograph: Melissa Mitchell
© Author Photograph: Silvija Lane

The moral right of the authors has been asserted.

ISBN 9978-1-912524-78-5

ECHECS AMOUREUX

What can they do but advance,
the stone pawns of the heart,
and in love or indifference
take one another apart
with a ritual elegance?

Partners and adversaries
move pieces in silence,
and balance by contraries
their stratagems of defence.
So there can be no victories

in these courteous, slow dances
over the stricken board
till we steady our glances,
quicken, and make heard
the bold heart, taking its chances.

from: John Gohorry, *FIVE POEMS*, The Kit-Cat Press, 1977

CONTENTS

Introduction	1

1: VOYAGING ROUND THE MOON

A Remarkable Interview	4
The Truth About the Past	5
Remembering Don Smith/John Gohorry: George Szirtes	7
from A Little Bestiary	11
Re-imaging The Winter's Tale: John Gohorry's 'The Coast of Bohemia' and its tradition: Glyn Pursglove	13
from The Coast of Bohemia	19

2: WORK IN THE BUILDING GOES ON

What Managers Know	22
Stephanie Norgate considers A Manager's Dog	23
from A Manager's Dog	24

3: NEW LANGUAGES

Talk into the Late Evening	28
On the Edge	29
About Time	30
from Terra Damnata	31
Samuel Johnson's Amber: Stuart Henson	32
V MacPherson	33
XXIX The Touch	34
XI Second Strophe: The Liar	36

4: THE SINGING BOWL

A Singing Bowl	40

Forty-Eight Gates: Peter Bennet	44
from Forty-Eight Gates	47

5: CONJECTURAL MUSIK

The Gohorry Double: John Greening	50
from Hölderlin at the Piano	56

6: HEAR-NO-GOOD, SEE-NO-GOOD, TELL-YOU-NO-LIES

Among the Yahoos: Stuart Henson	60
Briefings	64
Rougue Houyhnhnm	67
Garafe in the Houyhnhnms' Assembly	68
Gulliver Among the Houyhnhnms	69
The Public Poet: Merryn Williams	70
Augustan	70
His Doubt Tree	73
Pandemic	75
A Sunset Meditation	76
The Stock Exchange of Ideas: David Van-Cauter	78
The Stock Exchange of Ideas	82
The Spinney	83

7: OUT OF THE FIRE ROOM

The Fire Room	86
Pattern & Purpose: John Lane	88
Lost	94
An Admirer of Francis Ponge Revisits Holcombe, Devon: John Gohorry	96
An Invented Man	101
Biography	103
Bibliography	105

INTRODUCTION

Stuart Henson, May 2022

If you've picked up this volume, the chances are that you knew John Gohorry and own some of his books—or that you didn't, but something has intrigued you, his name perhaps, his reputation, and you're curious to find out more. In either case, *Bold Heart* is intended for you. When John died suddenly in October 2021, it felt as if a force had gone out of the world—a force for good, for humane understanding, for life itself. This book, then, is intended not only as a tribute, bringing together essays and reviews from a number of fellow-writers, but also as an introduction to his work, gathering some three dozen of his poems including several from the collection he was working on at the time of his death.

John Gohorry is, of course, a pen-name, the one he signed inside his books—the name I knew first and which, for consistency, is used in most of the essays here. Those who knew Don Smith, born in Coventry in 1943, student at University College London, Lecturer at North Hertfordshire College, the friend, teacher and family man, will have to forgive us: it's a duality that's just one (or two) facet(s) of a hugely energetic personality.

He wrote his M.Phil. on *The Sources & Style of Sydney's Arcadia*, and in many ways John Gohorry is the genuine Renaissance Man. His historical knowledge and his linguistic exuberance, distilled in his great long poems, 'Samuel Johnson's Amber', 'The Age of Saturn' and 'Impromptus for George Erdmann', are evident everywhere in his work. But he was no dry academic: the settings, the characters, of his imagination, live in worlds transmuted by a lyrical tenderness and illuminated by the white light of his intelligence.

He was also a man possessed of a real sense of fun, and that can be seen in the sheer bravura of his comic and satirical poems—and in the 'Multimedia Experiments' he published on YouTube in the years between 2009 and 2015. They're still there, under his Don Smith title, and I'd recommend the

Wagneresque venture into *The Car Wash* for a genuine multimedia experience. He was a teacher, a guide and a mentor—and something of a Zen philosopher. A link from his website will take you to a recording of John reading his poem 'The Singing Bowl', matched with video of the sage himself, seated among bamboos on his beloved Isle de Ré and striking the Singing Bowl at appropriate intervals.

In this gathering of appreciations, individual poems and excerpts, I've tried to follow the logic of John Gohorry's works and provide a sampler of them. He published many poems in pamphlet form, collecting them later along with newer pieces in volumes like *A Voyage Round the Moon* and *The Age of Saturn*. The bibliography on page 105 is intended to provide the reader with a guide to what may be found, both in and out of print. The fourteen books and numerous pamphlets bear witness to his prodigious energy. To read them is to go on wonderful journeys, to places and times not always familiar—yet all his.

My thanks are due to everyone who has so generously contributed to this volume. The selection of John's poems has been guided by them but is, in the end, my own.

1: Voyaging Round the Moon

A REMARKABLE INTERVIEW

Five Doctor Watsons called that afternoon
at the Baker Street lodgings; men of identical build,
age, and character, it appeared, all skilled

personators, candidates for the vacancy.
Holmes sat in his leather-buttoned chair and smoked;
the interviewees entered singly, each one cloaked

in secrecy. They had read *Strand Magazine*
and knew the profile backwards. Greatcoat, spats,
moustache, black bag, the Army background that's

unfakeable—they had all these by heart.
Holmes questioned carefully. Which of the five cloned
characters must be discarded, and which owned

to as Doctor Watson? The first was far too shrewd,
the second not polite enough to Mrs Hudson.
The third resembled Moriarty's godson

(some trick about the voice). As for the fourth,
there lurked behind his candid, open eyes
a stealth, a cunning he could not disguise.

When the fifth left, Holmes had met his match.
The perfect Watson! What followed, but begin
work on the partnership the pair were in

—and prove that he, too, could be genuine?

THE TRUTH ABOUT THE PAST

In the days that money was money and men were men
a pound was a week's wages, but then again
sixpence would pay for a night out on the town;
you could fly to New York for half a crown.
The most beautiful books imaginable cost a penny
and as for bus and train fares, there weren't any.
You could travel (on foot) free for five hundred miles;
to go further afield, people used bicycles.

My pocket money was a halfpenny a year
and, being extravagant, I spent somewhere near
a quarter of that on toys and expensive things
—the rest I put carefully into my bank savings.
I bought a Cadillac when I was twelve
for a shilling, and pedalled it myself
at a hundred and sixty through the garage doors
in a loud red blur and a haze of exhaust vapours.

There were no televisions then, and a radio
was something for attentive listening to;
the man read the news in a bowler hat,
a pressed white shirt, and a clean cravat
so his voice would be dignified too, and quite formal.
Ties matching pyjamas were perfectly normal
(I wore one myself). Sometimes I stayed up late
until half-past seven, or rarely, ten to eight.

Houses then were not like our present poky affairs
—they had thousands of rooms, and vertical stairs
stretching up higher than you'd ever have guessed
possible, almost as high as Mount Everest.
Gardens were huge land-masses mapped
by intrepid explorers, continents wrapped
in this mystery of tulips, or that impenetrable
overgrowth, green, butterfly haunted, and vegetable.

Potatoes burst out of the earth like fat coins;
sunworshipping deckchair marrows varnished their loins
in the tropical heat; beans heaved, dangled and shook
to overweight bees bringing fresh insects to cook
in their scarlet ovens. Perpendicular rain
sluiced out of overblown thunderbags to drain
down sheer cliffs of cabbagesides, daffodils
struck by lightning, sodden, drowned molehills.

Appetites were enormous with six cooked dishes
a day, and between meals sandwiches
thicker than haystacks layered with solid breeze-
blocks of butter, tomatoes and cucumber. Cheese-
burgers crowded with onions like an aircraft hanger
on Exhibition Day kept off the edge of hunger.
Thirst was proportionate of course, and I drank
bathfuls of cocoa, tea from the storage tank.

And in the old days, finally, habits were different;
gentle talk resolved people's differences, not argument,
bitter quarrels, a violent punch on a sore head,
armies in uniform, rifles, a nuclear warhead.
Proverbs and tender love songs were everyone's language
and just the right words for an imaginable golden age.
We listened to one another, and sat up straight,
told the truth always, did not exaggerate.

REMEMBERING DON SMITH/JOHN GOHORRY

George Szirtes

We moved to Hitchin in autumn 1973, the year I graduated from Goldsmiths with a teaching certificate after four previous years at art school. Hitchin was the home of my wife, Clarissa's parents and they had an available house that had been accommodating American servicemen. Clarissa was pregnant with our first child and I had found a part-time job as an art teacher at Cheshunt some two hours journey away by public transport and, looking for a little more work, took up a class at Hitchin College which is where I first met Don Smith, later – or rather, alternatively – known as John Gohorry. I had also found our nearest local poet, Roger Burford Mason, who lived just round the corner.

This opened up a small community of poets in Hitchin and Hertfordshire generally. Roger had learned typesetting from two other poets, Peter Scupham and John Mole who, together, ran the Mandeville Press, also in town. Roger then taught me, and I met Peter and John shortly after. I think Don must have learned from Roger as I had, though possibly a little later. Roger started the Dodman Press (*dodman* is the Norfolk word for snail). Through Roger I also met John Cotton and Freda Downie who both lived in Berkhamsted, not too far away. They in turn introduced us to others.

What facilitated all this private printing was that technology was rapidly changing and smaller printers were getting rid of their monotype fonts and the relevant presses at very low cost. Each of the presses was doing something slightly different: Peter and John produced pamphlets for various poets, some very well known – Patric Dickinson, Anthony Hecht, John Fuller and Geoffrey Grigson among them – but also published first pamphlets by Freda Downie (soon to be published by Secker as John already was, and I was to join them there). Peter already had a first book from OUP and was the best known of us. Clarissa and I founded The Starwheel Press on the basis of a large motorised letterpress and an Edwardian etching press to produce portfolios of etchings and new poems by various artists and poets. Roger too published poems, including my pamphlet, *The Iron Clouds* in 1974 and Don's *Castle Acre Priory* in 1978 but he was also interested in printing tradition and production in themselves. He also founded and edited the magazine Grand Piano, where many including Don and I appeared. John Cotton's Priapus press had begun with a magazine before then and also produced booklets of poems with or without pictures.

All these presses overlapped in some ways, selling poetry chiefly through subscription. They also generated new poets, new readings, and new reading circuits. Roger was particularly concerned with Don and me and we would drive to venues together, Don as John Gohorry. Roger's energy was central to this at that time as I doubt whether either Don or I would have had the social confidence to set up such arrangements. I can't remember how often I read with Don, with or without Roger, but there would have been a number of occasions.

Nearly all the poets were teachers of one kind or another. Don was teaching English at Hitchin College, Roger at one of the two Hitchin girls' schools and I at the other, the one that had been a grammar, where I was teaching art and art history. Roger's dynamism extended to founding a jazz group in which he played saxophone and I was on the piano. Don wasn't a part of that.

Of the three of us, Roger, Don and me, Don was the most overtly scholarly in his poetry. There was, indeed, a mild scholarly air about him. He spoke quietly and calmly, his poetry founded on learning, wit and a judicious understanding of form. His poems, at that stage, had a wry, proverbial quality that was expanding into philosophical exploration. I myself was learning to use verse forms but I came from a more surreally inclined art school background that found expression in instinctive visual imagery.

We all had young families and did meet as families on occasion. Since Roger lived just a street away it was easier for us to meet more frequently, though we did see Don's family – his first wife Judy and their children Ben, Zoë and Claire – on occasion. He was to experience a tragedy soon with a cot death that led a little later to the break-up of the marriage.

None of us was a regular pub goer so there were no organised meetings at this or that bar and there was never a Hitchin or Hertfordshire group as such where we could mutually discuss our poems in progress. We met on an individual ad hoc basis and, rarely, to discuss poems. Roger might pop round to us or I to Roger's and show a new poem but there was nothing regular about it. I might, also – after 1975 – drop in to Peter to show him a poem (and, later, he might show me a new one of his) but this was infrequent. We were, after all, full time teachers with young children, and our jobs and families would have consumed quite a lot of evening time. I don't think any of us, except perhaps Roger, were great socialisers. Peter and I were writing and producing plays at our respective schools and, bar seeing a few friends, that was as social as we got.

In 1978 I was chosen to be in Faber's Poetry Introduction 4, which then led to my first book with Secker and Warburg in 1979 so Peter, John Mole, Freda and I were with major publishers. Don was to find a first home with Harry Chambers' splendid Peterloo Press (who were also the first publishers of U A Fanthorpe, among many others.) So, by the 80s, there we were, all with books.

I am not sure at what point Don met Gerlinde. There might have been an earlier connection, but they came together after Judy, Don's first wife, left him. Together, they moved to Letchworth and we saw them less frequently although I did see Don's poems when they appeared. I myself organised readings at Hitchin library and for the Hitchin Festival at a local wine bar. Don would have read there along with poets from various parts of the country.

In 1988 Roger and his family moved to Toronto and Roger quickly made a reputation there as editor, short story writer and broadcaster but was to die there, far too early, of cancer. It was a shock for a man of such outgoing energy. He and Don were very close by then and Don flew out for the funeral. I was asked to write a poem and did so. I had changed school by then, had moved to Norfolk where I had another job, and had published more books. We exchanged Christmas cards with news every year but weren't in personal touch.

    I did do a reading for Don a few years ago. He looked much the same and was as friendly and jovial as ever. He had of course published a good deal more by then, latterly with the Shoestring Press and won a number of prizes including the Keats/Shelley Prize in 2008. There had been a considerable lacuna in collections – though not individual poems in magazines and prizes – between his second Peterloo book, *Talk Into the Late Evening*, which was a PBS Recommendation, in 1992 and his first from Shoestring in 2009, but a more than steady stream after that.

    I think now there was something else beside civilised scholarly wit, wisdom and grace in Don's poetry, though these are rare and precious gifts in themselves, especially in the times we live in. Poetry, like sanity, needs an internal apprehension, an edginess of some kind. We need a restless ghost in the machine, to sense the chaos within the order. I think Don's poetry had that throughout though it was never dramatized or played up. The dark places of unreason haunt sanity and grace and, I think, Don was well aware of those places. They register on the pulse of his verse.

FROM A LITTLE BESTIARY

1 PARROT

Psittacus, preening himself on his high perch,
is a fine fellow for feathers or for declensio verbi;
for quis est puer pulcher vel pulchrior, search
hic et ubique, none has his quality.

Quaestiones antwortet er avec noch mehr Fragen,
eloquent arc-en-ciel in his silver cage;
Sapientia habet toujours etwas zu sagen
for the betterment of mankind, in any language.

Imitatio hominis, then, with your leather tongue
and your caput cocked sideways avec nonchalance,
teach us the true knowledge that is never sung,
the real wisdom, that is without significance.

2 SPIDER

Tarantula and black widow are exotic species,
tropical, and fatal in a crate of bananas,
but harmless and altogether domestic is this
homespun, familiar Euclid of the campanulas

weaving his slender threads from the blue flowers
of the chalklands, three denier to catch the wind,
yet so strong that even the preposterous gale tires
finally, drowsing in the net where he is skeined.

Sweep him from the stair corner, then, if sweep you must
this image of elegance, strength, sheer simplicity;
though happy the man who could spin out of his dust
half such an idle, magnificent web for posterity.

5 SNAKE

Serpent, that brought us out of paradise
twisted and hissing for our love of wrong,
you are the patron of oracles, sly advice,
the treacherous benefactor with the forked tongue.

At the despatchbox, and in the rumpled bed
where in the small hours voices of lovers meet,
your sinuous whisper qualifies what is said,
masking truth's sense of shame with bland deceit.

Go, snake, hide in the dust, for your vice
and the virtues we might be capable of should not mix;
hopeful perhaps one day to regain paradise,
faithful in love, truthful in politics.

RE-IMAGING THE WINTER'S TALE: JOHN GOHORRY'S 'THE COAST OF BOHEMIA' AND ITS TRADITION

Glyn Pursglove

A Voyage Round The Moon, (Harry Chambers/Peterloo Poets, 1985) contains – pp.68-74 – a sequence of ten poems: 'The Coast of Bohemia'. The title alludes to the opening of Act Three, Scene iii of Shakespeare's *The Winter's Tale*, when Antoninus asks a mariner, "Thou art perfect, then our ship hath touch'd upon/ The deserts of Bohemia?". As early as 1619 (Shakespeare's play was first acted *c*.1611 and published in 1623), Ben Jonson is reported to have told the Scottish poet William Drummond of Hawthornden, somewhat contemptuously, that "Shakespeare, in a play, brought in a number of men saying they had suffered shipwreck in Bohemia where there is no sea near by some 100 miles" (Ben Jonson, *The Complete Poems*, ed. G. Parfitt, 1975, p.466). This supposed geographical error by Shakespeare provoked much discussion in the 18th and 19th centuries; some explained that there *had* been short periods when Bohemia possessed land on the Adriatic coast, while others blamed the 'error' on incompetent printers. But the 'blunder' long fascinated pedantic scholars. Indeed, in 1910 a writer in *The Academy* (October 1, 1910, p.318) reported that "The 'Problem Editor' of the Westminster Gazette recently offered a prize for the best essay on 'The Sea Coast of Bohemia'". The 'coast of Bohemia' is, however, only one of several such 'errors' in the *Winter's Tale*. The play, after all, praises Giulio Romano's prowess as a sculptor when his fame was principally as a painter and architect and presents him as being active at the same time as the Oracle of Apollo at Delphi (or "Delphos" as Shakespeare calls it). In any case, where Bohemia was concerned Shakespeare was simply following one of his main sources for the play, Robert Greene's romance *Pandosto*, which speaks of "the coast of Bohemia".

A few had the wit to recognize the irrelevance of such questions. So, for example, William Archer, when surveying productions of *The Winter's Tale* (*The Nineteenth Century*, 128, October 1887) described it as a play "into which Shakespeare has deliberately crammed every impossibility of time, place and circumstance, lest anyone should mistake it for anything but a Winter's Tale, a *Wintermärchen*"; even more forcefully and earlier, the minor poet James Ellis had published (in *The Poetry of Real Life*, 1851) a sonnet *with a mischievously long title:* 'Against those critics who cavil at the unchronological juxtapositions of the old painters, and condemn a play of Shakespeare, because he represents Antigonus landing with Perdita on the Sea-Coast of Bohemia':

The Muse has other charts than yours—she has
Lands not yet marked, Hesperian isles (in vain
Sought for by ye) in Poesy's wide Main:

[…]

O happy, *happy* he, who with her sails,
Her compass true to the great pole of Truth,
Though, now and then, she deviate in details—
Through literal error reaching purest sooth,
She time and space at will doth join and change,
To give Truth universal wider range!

Geographical or historical accuracy are, of course, subordinate to another kind of 'truth' in works of the imagination. One proof that a work contains such 'truth' is that it stimulates further imaginative (re)creations by other artists. Some of Shakespeare's plays (such as such as *Hamlet, Romeo and Juliet* and *A Midsummer Night's Dream*) have provoked such re-imaginings on an almost industrial scale. Versions of *The Winter's Tale* have been less numerous, but John Gohorry has more than a few predecessors. There were at least two theatrical adaptations in the Eighteenth Century: David Garrick's *Florizel and Perdita* (1758) and *The Sheep-Shearing* (1777) by George Colman the Elder. Operatic versions have included Max Bruch's *Hermione* (1872), Karl Goldmark's *Ein Wintermärchen* (1908), John Harbison's *Winter's Tale* (1974) and Ryan Wigglesworth's *The*

Winter's Tale (2017). Of prose fiction written in response to *The Winter's Tale* the earliest work I know is by Mary Cowden Clarke (1809-98) a pioneering female Shakespeare scholar who, amongst much else, wrote a series of 15 stories under the general title of *The Girlhood of Shakespeare's Heroines*, published in three volumes between 1850 and 1852. The story entitled 'Hermione: The Russian Princess' was first published in 1852. It is some forty pages long, well imagined and organized. The story has several points of contact with the play: the moment (III.ii.119) when, at her trial, Hermione declares "The Emperor of Russia was my father" is only the most obvious of these. In 2015 Jeanette Winterson's *The Gap of Time* was published. Winterson's novelisation of Shakespeare's play is set in the USA and the UK, at a time close to the date of publication. Character names are naturally changed – the Leontes figure is now called 'Leo' and is a financier rather than a king. The novel's 'Hermione', 'MiMi' is a half-French singer and dancer. The 'Polixenes' is called Xeno. Overall Winterson's book displays a good deal of perception and wit, but there is very little 'poetry' left. Winterson's re-imaging is most striking when discussing gender and sexuality.

Until quite recently, the poems written in response to the *Winter's Tale* have been rather disappointing; such few Victorian examples as I have come across are very slight and don't merit discussion.

Successful poems from the Twentieth Century with which I am familiar include Louis MacNeice's 'Autolycus' (*Selected Poems*, 1964) – an astute observation on Autolycus's importance to the play –, Edwin Morgan's 'Instructions to an Actor' (*New Selected Poems*, 2000) and, of course, John Gohorry's 'The Coast of Bohemia'.

Edwin Morgan (characteristically) takes a very individual approach. His 'Instructions' present, by implication, the words of Shakespeare addressed to the boy actor who is the first interpreter of the role of Hermione. He is told that he will "stand on a pedestal behind a curtain,/ for eighty lines; don't move, don't speak, don't breathe./ I'll stun them all out there, I'll scare them,/ make them weep, but it depends on you" (*ll*. 2–6). There follow further details of how the 'business' of

Hermione's apparent revivification will be staged and the poem's closing lines capture the very real power it can (and should) have in the theatre: "you move, you step down, down from the pedestal,/ control your skirt with one hand, the other hand/ you now hold out – / O this will melt their hearts of nothing does – /to your husband who wronged you long ago / and hesitates in amazement/ to believe you are alive./ Finally he embraces you, and there's nothing/ I can give you to say, boy/ but you must show that you have forgiven him. The wonderful last two lines,

> Forgiveness, that's the thing. It's like a second life.
> I know you can do it. – Right then shall we try?

are surely directed to the reader as much, if not more, as the actor and might, indeed, be understand as the core of the play's meaning.

Gohorry's sequence is made up of ten poems: (1) 'In the Garden', (2) 'In Jail', (3) 'Return Journey', (4) 'Bears', (5) 'Time Rehearses his Entrance', (6) 'Gifts', (7) 'Aboard Ship', (8) 'Sitting it out', (9) 'Finis coronat opus' and (10) 'A Late Wedding'. Several, e.g. poems 1-5, 7-8 and 10 imagine situations alluded to in Shakespeare's text but not seen on stage. However, there is throughout a strong sense of theatrical performance as, for example, in 'Gifts':

> Perdita's shock of flowers is all plastic
> no doubt, but for that none the less real

or the closing lines of 'A Late Wedding':

> Then applause breaks their reverie, and at once,
> Knowing what is expected, they take hands and dance.

'In the Garden' has its origins in the first act of the play when, at Leontes' urging (I.ii.173-5) Hermione agrees to try to persuade Polixenes to stay longer in Sicily. She tells her husband (*ll*. 177-8) "If you would seek us,/ We are yours i' th' garden". Gohorry imagines the episode in the garden as a wholly decorous matter of courtly formalities – "Only the garden is witness to the formalities/ of their lovemaking. And they remain formal/ now, when exchanging the closer formalities/ seclusion allows.". What happens between Hermione and Polixenes is clearly 'courtesy', rather than 'courtship'. 'In Jail' presents Hermione in prison, after Leontes has ordered (*W.T.* II.i.103) "Away with her, to prison". Gohorry's Hermione "knows the extremities/ of deprivation". Her situation is universalized by an unspoken pun on the word 'confinement' in the poem's closing lines: "hers is the condition of all women/ – locked in a hot cell, straining for a grim birth." The 'return journey' of poem 3 is that made by Cleomenes and Dion, sent by Leontes (*W.T.*, II.i.182-86) "[t]o sacred Delphos, to Apollo's temple". The fourth poem 'Bears' alludes, of course, to the play's famous stage direction, 'Exit, pursued by a bear' (III.iii,58) and to Antigonus, eaten by a bear in, as Gohorry puts it, a "grizzly picnic". Yet the baby he was carrying was saved: "The hunched bears/ with their bad manners are cheated of the drenched/ innocent whom just this once Providence spares". 'Time Rehearses his Entrance' is a witty, perceptive monologue for the actor playing Time, who must deliver the crucial speech which opens Act IV and with it the second, redemptive 'movement' of *The Winter's Tale*: "I will be the illusion – state a fact/ or two to start off the remote fourth act, / give explanations, histories, a blessing,/ wind up the clock, exit, and leave them guessing". In a very effective touch, Gohorry ends the poem by quoting (italicized) the first lines of Time's speech – so that the rest of the poem seems to represent the actor's thoughts before going on stage. 'Gifts' is a sonnet reflecting on Act IV, scene iv of Shakespeare's play, in particular the episode in which Perdita distributes flowers to "the strangers"; it recognizes that "her gifts [...] mirror exactly what they feel" and affirms that "there is no faking/ her palpitating heart, whose strength implies/ love, that miraculous flower that never dies.". 'Aboard Ship' addresses the voyage from Bohemia to Sicily, proposed by Camillo in Act IV scene iv; the poem identifies the guiding principle of the play's phase of renewal: "the navigator, Love, who keeps the charts/ ear-marked and up to date with what each must/ perform routinely, Truthfully, the art's// doing as Love instructs – her power is/ to teach conditions otherwise untaught." In 'Sitting it out' we observe Hermione in "the cold chapel", the chapel referred to by Leontes at line 239 of Act III, scene ii, and in which the 'awakening' of Hermione from her statue will take place in Act V, scene iii. Fittingly, it is to that moment that Gohorry's next poem, 'Finis Coronat Opus' takes us. Many modern critics have explored the relationship between nature and art as a theme in Shakespeare's play but none, I think, have expressed its rich paradoxes as well as John Gohorry does:

> Even Julio Romano couldn't have managed this
> – past master of pitcher, gouge, and chisel;
> such a totally accomplished mimesis
> of nature by her ape art is unnatural.

But this moment, great as it is, isn't quite the end ("Finis") of Shakespeare's "Opus". The revivification of Hermione and Leontes' full recognition of his errors make yet more possible. Paulina, Hermione's most faithful friend, and widow of Antigonus is rewarded for her resilient fidelity by a new marriage, to Camillo, foolishly exiled by Leontes earlier. And, indeed, it is Leontes (hitherto the breaker of marriages) who creates this marriage (in the last speech of the play). There seems no reason to doubt that the wedding 'happens', as it were, after the play ends. Gohorry's presentation of it is delicate and touching: "Picture them stepping down to their wedding feast/ the greybeard, the widow of the bear's breakfast,/ without having met for over a decade/ but magically now brought to the marriage bed/ and beyond".

Of the literary re-imaginings of *The Winter's Tale*, this by John Gohorry seems to me the finest. It is the most comprehensive and the most imaginatively perceptive. In its verbal music, its wit and its psychological insight it celebrates the play's imaginative, moral and emotional coherence, as it affirms the 'truth' about 'the Coast of Bohemia'.

FROM THE COAST OF BOHEMIA

5 TIME REHEARSES HIS ENTRANCE

Being oneself is quite impossible.
I shall content myself with being plausible,
merely, decked out with the conventional props
—hourglass, and scythe. None of the humming tops,
rattles, and soft toys from the nursery
to give away young Time's identity,
but frowsty wig and itching beard I'll wear
to thicken up these infant tufts of hair,
and to disguise the innocence of youth
make play of my fictitious daughter, Truth.

I will be the illusion—state a fact
or two to start off the remote fourth act,
give explanations, histories, a blessing,
wind up the clock, exit, and leave them guessing,
concerned more to anticipate the next
development than penetrate my text,
whose secret function must be to disguise
Time's unendurable realities
with platitudes. For ordinary folk
rightly prefer a cliché to a joke
in bad taste played against them—confidence
is the best tonic for an audience.
I am the boy who died—what's in the mirror?

'I that please some, try all, both joy and terror
of good and bad, that makes and unfolds error.'

7 ABOARD SHIP

Hurriedly they embark; no preparation
delays their setting out with formal rules;
none of them needs to give an explanation,

stepping disguised aboard the Ship of Fools.

The ship speeds readily across the water,
evading pirates, customs-men, and Turks;
the tinsel Prince, the lion-tamer's daughter,
the circus manager, the Clerk of Works,

King Mutton, and his mythopoeic son
take turns at steering. And the voyage will end
auspiciously, having so well begun
with everyone on deck, willing to lend

a hand to getting there if they can trust
the navigator, Love, who keeps the charts
ear-marked and up to date with what each must
perform routinely. Truthfully, the art's

doing as Love instructs—her power is
to teach conditions otherwise untaught.
Now they shake out their fresh identities;
their boat sinks, and they vanish through the port.

9 FINIS CORONAT OPUS

Even Julio Romano couldn't have managed this
—past master of pitcher, gouge, and chisel;
such a totally accomplished mimesis
of nature by her ape art is unnatural.

The wrinkles chipped in her smooth brow
lifelikely seem to furrow and wreathe
as if she were puzzled—curious to know
how after all these years she might breathe

and embrace him again, as now she does
gingerly, for fear of her wet paint.
Their lips touch in a tentative purpose,
full of tenderness life might invent.

2: Work in the Building Goes On

John Gohorry turned his satirical eye to the politics of the workplace at several points in his career, most notably in the early pamphlet 'A Lecturing Life', (1986) which was praised by Peter Porter in The Observer, *and later reproduced in* The Age of Saturn.

'What Managers Know' appeared in another of his self-published pamphlets Arcadian Silver *(1998)*

WHAT MANAGERS KNOW

The exact height of a staircase; how long the lifts
take between floors; ex-directory numbers;

the onus of taking charge; the satisfactions
of consulting, of being right; the procedures

that will bring about a decision, or relegate it
to the tomorrows of committee and working party;

the fragrance of secretaries, whose pale hands
bring coffee and biscuits, agendas, consolations;

the pleasures of working late. And, after hours,
the darkness that falls in corridors, the darkness

that falls over the heart in the bleak interval
before going home, after the cleaners come.

STEPHANIE NORGATE CONSIDERS A MANAGER'S DOG (POETRY REVIEW, VOL. 102/2 SUMMER 2012)

…John Gohorry's pamphlet *A Manager's Dog*, is also allusive, taking off from an epigram by Pope. In this traditional satire, with its references to animals, power structures and empty materialism, Fido recounts his master's changing fortunes in a variety of metres. Despite the cutting satire, an appreciation of our dependency on dogs gleams through, 'Dogs sift through the debris, their sense/alert to the least sign of life/eyes, nose, and ears attuned perfectly/to the pitch of human survival.' The final female villainy might not be missed, though Juvenal would approve; otherwise, as they say of novels, I couldn't put this down.

FROM A MANAGER'S DOG

I

He calls me Fido, which in Latin means
I am faithful. Faithful is what
he wants me to be, above all;
(had he named me *Rocky* or *Fuse*
I would have known that he prized,
in the first instance, massive strength,
in the second, explosive aggression).

He has thoroughly trained me.
I sit, fetch, wait, walk, find, stand guard,
watch, hold, come to heel,
and all at a word.

Work in the building goes on;
at the top, the directors
with windows that catch the light
from the ends of the earth;
at the bottom, men covered in grease.
We're in the middle, for now.

He has plans, an agenda.
Some of its steps are open, some secret.
I do whatever he wants.

I do it at once, as he orders.
Faithful is what I am.

VII

All week I spent prowling
the sheds, looking for Weak Ones.
Already, he said, he had names;
what he wanted was confirmation

or the opposite, based on gut feeling,
another expression for sixth sense,
or a dog's smell for what's right.

So I nosed around men
covered in grease, keen to distinguish
those for whom grease is cosmetic
from those for whom it's a concomitant
of productive work, trailed women
through the solvent-sweet paintshops
looking for workers with hands
smelling too much of laundry, earlobes
unflecked by paint smudges.

I herded them into a great pen
with a wicket at one end,
drove them through one at a time
to go head to head with the others.
He sat among the selectors,
grim-faced, full of solicitude.

They praised him, when it was over,
for his resilience, his capacity
to make hard decisions.

They had him ear-marked for greatness.
They said he had far to go.

IX

In the new age, I have additional
roles, and a new collar.

It is made of camelskin, cut
from an animal slaughtered on purpose
for the production of collars.

The skin lay for a year
on the thigh of an olive-skinned virgin
who kneaded it daily.

It fits my neck, soft as wax.

My leash is a single, unbelievably
long strand of silk, gossamer fine,
along which I can feel every pulse
from the nerves of his fingers.

I stand guard in his doorway,
his gatekeeper, admitting, excluding,
detaining, his minder, 24/7.

I know all who call by their smell,
which I do not forget.

I've not yet
had human blood in my mouth.

When the time comes
I will do what I should.

3: New Languages

TALK INTO THE LATE EVENING

They are slowly falling asleep at last in the wicker nursery,
bears, blossoms and comforters strewn over their counterpanes
while the inexhaustible summer sunlight still improvises a dance

through the appletrees, and their curtains turn distant lands
hailed through the yellow roomshine by their explorers' vowels;
Cra-croucrou, they are calling, *toohou, cacrou, toutou, toohou.*

Downstairs, there are bright adult sallies of arrival and greeting
—laughter—*Oh, those magnificent flowers! Fetch a vase, darling!*
bubbles the hostess, then—*What a beautiful dress you are wearing!*

from the fragrant male guests fluttering to her candle flame.
And later, when the wineglasses are emptied and the cutlery clatters
over the smoothed tablecloth, there is the stridor of small talk

growing more serious until night thickens in the laurel bushes
and the dinner party projects itself through the open windows
in a corona of yellow light out onto the fold-aways of the lawn.

Upstairs, the far countries have slipped into a short silence;
but making their goodnight calls at the gate under a white moon
they keep an ear open for new languages, slowly becoming theirs.

ON THE EDGE

Hogan, a footman, pulled her out of the early morning
water, the park being generally deserted, and himself
jilted the night before having thought of ending it all
in the same way, but reprieved. She floated towards him

unseasonable as a flowering lily in the December frost
which made the lake sparkle, her skirts spread wide,
their drenched fabric forming a rondel about her head.
He knew her for a respectable lady, her hands neatly

manicured and an expensive ring on her marriage finger;
it shone still. Then he saw under her heart the bunched
tumulus, put his hand hopelessly on the drowned satin.
He called out and the lake froze as they drew her away.

ABOUT TIME

If time is of the essence,
there's no time now for tedious prologues.
We must go straight to the heart of the matter.

If time is money,
we must make time for ourselves as we can,
spend our time wisely together.

If time allows,
there's no need to make allowances. Everything
will come right in the nick of time.

If time will tell,
our thoughts one day will become public knowledge.
How then should we carry the burden of secrets?

If time will serve,
do we still need to worry about tomorrow?
Today, you and I have all the time in the world.

FROM TERRA DAMNATA

A SEASONAL LAMENT

She lay all in teen by the wilger tree
—twangdillow, twangdillow, what does she vizy?

her prew Dametas now all turned gullion,
the faithless swingebreech, gone with another.

That scowbanker enamorato with his flim-flam villanellas
made love out of shuffs merely, poor kickshiwinshes;

she weighs love on the ansellshaft, and her heart is heavy.
Weariness now is her shotclog, sorrow her dole.

A FASHIONABLE PAIR

Here's Sharnbud, a privisant, tall man, her sweetakin,
sporting his brand new drabdrubbery and silk famblers,

and on his arm Spigurnel all lah-di-dah farthingale
and mantled fontanges, a proper nicebecetur.

The clapperdudgeons bait them in envious scoggery
—call him true prickmedainty, mamuque, popingoe,

and her marsheet, pompardy-monger, simper-de-cocket.
But they pass by, heads erect, girned by such tediouste.

SAMUEL JOHNSON'S AMBER

Stuart Henson

Sometimes you felt John Gohorry's was an Eighteenth Century imagination let loose on the Twenty-first Century. He didn't just write books; he *invented* them. The world as he saw it was teeming with characters, bursting with potential to delight and surprise. What first convinced me that he was a genius was reading, or attempting to read, *Samuel Johnson's Amber*. When it came out in 2010, it didn't receive the attention it warranted. I remember talking about it with his publisher, John Lucas, who observed wryly that the reviewers and literary editors were too easily daunted by its size and scope. It's a book to grapple with and to relish for the exuberance of its language, its willingness to entertain—and, it must be said, occasionally to puzzle.

In broadest terms, it enquires into the life of Samuel Johnson in the years when he was composing his dictionary, and enters into a kind of dialogue with him through the persona of an imagined anti-Johnsonian personality—the 'outsider' Malachi Macpherson. One of the joys of the book is John's extensive, and, I believe, entirely un-ironic Introduction, in which he explains his intention in creating this figure:

'What I wanted to explore was language itself, in which Johnson, or perhaps better, a Johnsonian principle, represented one axis or dimension of value and against which I set out to oppose another, originally conceived of as its opposite in every way. Where the Johnsonian principle exemplified such qualities as truth, order and judicious differentiation, the other would embody falsehood, disorder and convergence. ... Where the Johnsonian principle exalted text, the other would exalt the spoken word. Where the Johnsonian principle was without music (Johnson was entirely unmusical), the other would be lyrical. And where the Johnsonian principle was English with Classical antecedents, the other would be non-English (I thought probably Scots, since Johnson had such an ambivalent attitude towards the Scots.)' The two lives weave in and out but they meet only once—on a coach journey, Macpherson appearing under alternative names such as Malarkey and Bagpipe. In true Johnson style, (perhaps he *is* being a little tongue-in-cheek here) John Gohorry declares that 'his name, which corrupts rapidly, has etymological links with *Fausen, a small eel*, and this character is, as the name implies, slippery and elusive… His language is a hybrid of Synthetic Scots, formed from the best I could fashion out of reading Burns, MacDiarmid, Dunbar and Henryson.' Here he is in poem five from the sequence:

V MACPHERSON

That was his name. Macpherson. MacFearson, the son
of Pherson, or Fearson, or Farson, the son of Far.
Ha' was nae gaberlunzie, the auld da, askand for aumous,
but a guid caird, and a sicker, fremit frae giglottis.
His was a queir, clatterin' taulk athegether, gabbin' Romanay.

Tracking his way soundlessly down the staircase of leaves
he senses how daylight fades, its gradual weakening;
he was the young son carried around in the rattling budgets
reading the roadways, melting away into the hedgerows.
And how raithly now maun ha' word to his ane fatherheid?

And quhat sall his barne be, his barne blithe and bonny?
Time sweetens its wound in the heart; the wood is his darkness
where mavis and merle whistle secret, accustomed songs;
ha' had songis for tocher quan ha' weddit the laundry lass
and ne'er a bodle besides. So he treads to his true love,

his breath fleeting outwards onto the chilly September air
amid flurries of silver cloud. He rounes table and measure,
the calculi of his hard earning hands and her maiden name
in snatches of improvised song. *O Mary McCarron, lemane mine*
– he turns her name over and over again like a bright coin.

A low gleid from the window; she has taken the shawls in,
the high, rolling curve of the sheets resolved at their fireside.

His hand on the latch. They embrace, making fresh discoveries.
Their wordis skelter doun right fra' the brugh o' the moon,
droppand into their just placis, like birds set for the night.

Words, dialogue, talk… these are constant preoccupations in *Samuel Johnson's Amber*, and Malachi's love-making very often implies both meanings of the expression. In poem thirty-seven, 'Strategies for Coherence', John Gohorry unwinds the metaphor further: 'They have come together, the man's / tongue and the woman's tongue… to contrive ecstasies which in the darkness / that they have joined remain interior discourses… They manoeuvre together, in folds, surges, / tugs and submissions, trips, juxts, and adverses; each moulding / its own rhythms to those of the other, so that in a short time / there is no other, but an integral understanding…'

Sometimes it's difficult to be certain whose voice is whose. Johnson, Macpherson, Gohorry… Indeed, there's a good deal of overlap between the authorial and dramatized voices. In the course of our correspondence, John Lane has mentioned to me a memoir that Don/John wrote eight years before the publication of *Samuel Johnson's Amber*. It concerned his aunt and uncle, and opened with the sentence 'No-one will ever now know for certain the identity of the lady who stood with her back to the darkness in a house on the eastern outskirts of Coventry one bitter winter's evening…' After describing the falling snow, the first paragraph closes with a striking recollection: 'she looked at me and said with great tenderness, *Goodbye my dear. I shall never see you again.*' It was with a ghostly shudder that I realised that the poem I had quite independently selected to represent Samuel Johnson's viewpoint in this book was number twenty-nine, one of two entitled 'The touch'.

XXIX THE TOUCH

As night fell, snow was already drifting steadily onto the fields at the back of the house, and the house itself had turned into a mauve breathing mound, its trees and outhouses levelling into an unmarked, compounded surface that was neither land, sky, nor water, but a cold, crystalline uniformity, silent and lovely.

The world was transforming itself, a few flakes at a time. Rose bushes thickened, ditches filled themselves in; the watercourses solidified, hillocks inflated their sides to a low, lowering moon breathing confidences into the blue air. Inside the house, a boy woke from a bad dream around midnight and stumbled downstairs;

he saw ice inside the windows, snow packing against the transoms and suddenly it was as if the inside and the outside of the house were the same. Birds huddled shivering in picture-frame corners which contained scenes of winter – a fox hiding behind his glass, and the mail-coach, crimson and black, rocking in eerie silence,

its occupants indistinct figures wrapped up in winter greatcoats. *The mantel was an ice precipice on which time itself had frozen.* The front door of the house blew open and a lady stood there as he squatted to ease himself; snow gusted down from the darkness at the back of her coat, and he knew both that he knew her and that

something immense was occurring, though in years afterwards he could never hatch further particulars. *Even then he was unable to tell whether this lady in coat, hat, handbag and winter shoes was passing into or out of the house.* She bent down to him, and with a touch of extreme tenderness kissed him on the forehead;

Good bye, my dear, were her exact words; *I shall never see you again.* The moment dissolved itself soon into his resumed sleep; snow drifted long after the moon withdrew from the hillside's confessions. He never did see her again, though when once more time gathered pace on the mantel, and the picture-frames, rotten

with age had been cast into bonfires, her goodbye wakened within him, after a long hibernation, its ambiguities still unresolved, its significance still incomplete and perhaps, because of that, resonant; the strong, distant, gravitational pull of the memory; gestures of parting; kindness; the world in its transformations.

There are so many wonderful, liminal things going on in this poem it would take an essay in itself to unpack them all. The mysterious farewell recurs later in the sequence, as part of the long exchange of 'Conversations in a Coach', this time on the lips of the spirit-character Green Jean and again in a snowy, dream-like context. And this just before a couple of Flaubertian 'grotesques' invade the space of the coach/poem and begin to babble phonemes and nonsense words. Johnson and Macpherson are seen to react in characteristically different ways to their incoherencies. If you weren't paying attention, these pages might begin to look like gobbledygook. In fact, they form part of a key section of a book that revels in the mysteries of language, where words glow and resonate, and ideas are embedded like creatures in amber resin.

John's introduction also makes clear that he intended to create a multi-layered post-modern work, one in which there are poems—strophes—commenting on, illuminating, the progress of the sequence itself. Again it's a luxury to quote in full here, but the second of these tells more about the process than any amount of exegesis could:

XI SECOND STROPHE: THE LIAR

How to describe the ways in which texture becomes text
when text must fold into itself in its own reflex,
be, itself, medium of disclosure?

The paradox of the liar was that he told the truth
when he described himself as a liar.

And who would forge the poem of textures – velvet,
mahogany – would never attain the two-tone continuum
in which texture is metaphorical.

Inside the bubble of air there was a human figure
and in the human figure, a breath.

Could one work backwards, perhaps, from the script?
Backwards to scripture, the dissolution of text
into fragments, its first coherencies?

The figure did not dissolve; it did not diminish.
It reached outwards augmenting itself.

These may be questions of boundaries. The single line
once drawn, and wherever drawn, generates cis
in the foreground, trans in the farground.

The line is pure energy pulsed
from the word to the man in the air-bubble

from the heart of the naming imagination, giving a name
which is throwing or spinning a line. The verse
crosses boundaries, works towards new limits.

The poet bursts out of his air-jacket; from his mouth
issues a formed breath, a name, certain new words.

The philosophical conundrum of the lying truth-teller returns again in 'The Fallacy of the Doorkeepers' in *Exploring Psalmanazar*. Everything folds back into itself. It took John Gohorry thirty years to bring *Samuel Johnson's Amber* fully into being. It's a huge work. (And I haven't even mentioned the mind-boggling, surrealist 'acruciferbostics') One day it will be the subject of someone's PhD thesis. Meanwhile there are copies to be found using the internet. If you haven't got one, hurry. If you do have one, hang on to it: you're already in possession of one of the great works of twenty-first century literature.

4: The Singing Bowl

A SINGING BOWL

1

What name will you give
to what strikes the singing bowl?
As all sounds are one
so the particular name
of what strikes the singing bowl

—*wand, mallet, birch-peg*—
fits the striker's intention
with what comes to hand
yet the striker's intention
does not strike the singing bowl.

2

What has the striker
to do with the world of names
now he approaches
the rim of the singing bowl
and with the least of touches

propounds a bell-note?
Who should he be but the one
sounding the bell-note,
set apart from the rapture
of all names, even his own?

3

Hammer blows fashioned
the curve of the singing bowl;
the coppersmith's ear
rang with the might-have-been notes

that his anvil discarded.

The bowl took them up,
held them over and under
the note he sounded;
it was as though metal sang
of strata where it was mined.

4

Voices of copper,
tin, zinc, manganese, nickel,
transition metals
from whose madrigal orbits
choirs of electrons compose

mind's sense of itself
as one note of music, whole,
resonant, fractalled
through time and space, that a touch,
vibrant and strong, sets ringing.

5

Before you struck it
you were a thousand actions
the bowl remembered
the way memory struggles
to know what it truly knows.

But now you strike it
the bowl sums up who you are
in a single note,
the DNA of a life
reckoned unerringly yours.

6

Its first song unschooled
by the process of singing,
it's said a bowl learns
articulation of notes,
the projection and carry

of pitch, tone, cadence,
chime, dissolution, until,
each note augmenting
the rest, to your inner ear
it sings of enlightenment.

7

The bowl sings, and you
whom it hardly imagined
take shape and structure,
an embryo self become
for as long as the note lasts

a person with form,
attitude, history. The bowl
is past and future;
its song, centuries old, fades
over nine months, and you're born.

8

With time, the bowl gains
patinas of carbonate,
red and black oxide,
as, mellow with age, it sings
a note augmented by time.

Transition evolves
to become transformation;
how wise is metal?
And what's your name, hearing it
ring true now for the first time?

FORTY-EIGHT GATES

Peter Bennet

This book is a remarkable achievement, and to be recommended to Western students of Zen traditions as well as to discerning readers of contemporary poetry. John Gohorry's forty-eight gates are, of course, also poems. Each one is in a short form, new to me, consisting of two stanzas, both of which are haikus which have been given two additional seven-syllable lines. This form allows him to suggest that the poems open and shut, as gates do, or even, as rather seems to be the case here, stand ajar. As the preface to the book puts it, gates may be opened gently or with force, some may need a locksmith, others can be left shut and climbed over. These poems are in fact engagements with the forty-eight koans compiled in 1228 by the Zen monk Mumon Ekai, and known collectively as *The Gateless Gate*. The original title therefore suggests that the gates are simultaneously both closed and open. As Gohorry says, all we need to do is walk through.

There are certainly ambiguities at work here, but not of language. The vocabulary of these poems is that of common usage and common sense, and no dictionary will be needed by the average English-speaking reader. There are no complexities of syntax. Familiar objects abound: walls, jugs, shadows, ribbons, cars and carts, mountains and molehills, trees, fungi, cats and foxes, flagpoles, a sack of potatoes, and of course the Buddha's shit-stick.

But what is happening? A collection of koans, Gohorry tells us, is like a mental gymnasium in which the Zen student can train. And these poems are the results of his work-outs in Mumon's gym. If that sounds a bit over-taxing, we are not to worry. The poems, he assures us, are sufficiently referenced both to their cultural context and to the common humanity of author and reader. And that, I think, is a true claim. Nevertheless, we have work to do. We are introduced, for example, or rather not introduced, to a big cast of characters, named but not otherwise identified, with whose activities and preoccupations the poems are concerned. Hyakujo, Seizei, Tokusan, Ummon, Joshu, Daruma, Shuzan, and many others, make their appearances and go on their way, without a hint of individuality or personality beyond the flash of actuality carried by the poem. What are we to make of them all? Do we need to know who they are or were? These are, I suspect, the wrong questions.

Because the poems are all the same shape and size the reader can half close his or her eyes and seem to see the same one on each page. This is of course by no means the case. Things happen. A fan waves in front of us, food is chewed toothlessly, shadows fall, a staff of office is snapped, a buffalo blocks the view from a window, breakfast is served. Reassertion of the same form does, however, make reading the book an unusual experience, and contributes substantially to its impact, which we can be sure is what Gohorry intends. But to repeat, what is happening? The word engagement has been chosen carefully. Although these poems are all derived from Mumon's koans, we are not being given translations, or overdrafts of translations, but rather encapsulations of experience, which seem to take place not in retrospect, but in a shared ever-present time of almost-glimpsed enlightenment. We are eavesdropping on a series of meditative psychodramas.

We are also not being offered the variety of appearance and intention we would normally expect in a collection. The poems in *Forty-Eight Gates* are all hitting the same target in different ways. Re-reading the book, to me, is not unlike walking through an exhibition of small kinetic sculptures. We pause in front of them. They perform their movements and engage us. We move on, pleased by what we have experienced, slightly bewildered. Quite often we go back and watch again, and when we do we are likely to be surprised to find that we are looking at ourselves in that very process of absorption and reflection. In a way this seems to be what the poems themselves are doing. This is one of the triumphs of the book. Take, for example, 'Your Mind is Moving': 'The flag does not move / in the wind that is moving; / the wind does not move / and the flag flies from its staff; / it is the mind that is moving. // Now the air is still. / The flag is without motion / limp by the flagpole. / Sitting there, thumbs together / how will you stop your mind moving?' If one of the things we value about poetry is the ability it has to make us look again with more delight as a result of sharing a writer's attention, and in my case it is, then where are we here? What is the focus of this poem's attention and therefore of ours? In 'The Sound of a Bell' it would seem to be any attempt at perception: 'The sound of a bell. / Does it travel towards you? / Does your ear grasp it / at source? How do you know it / for the bell-sound that it is? // And now the bell sounds / why break off meditation, / wrapping your mind up / in seven awarenesses / to travel the big wide world?' In 'Joshu's Oak Tree' the focus would seem to be meaning itself: 'Is meaning an oak? / It grows, branches and shelters / from small beginnings. / Daruma sails for China / and his frail craft is a reed. // A long time ago. / Will you sit and consider? / Your thoughts are songbirds. / Inbreath and outbreath. Observe / the oak tree in the garden.'

I have a feeling that the Zen masters themselves would approve the writer's achievement here in placing himself at a crucial remove from his material. We have no sense of John Gohorry's presence, no insistent voice, no autobiography or flights of fancy, no opinions, digressions, or wasted words. The material is presented to him by Mumon and he epitomises it for our enjoyment and, dare one say, instruction. These are consequently poems that pull much more than their own weight. They are exemplary, both in insight and economy, and a joy to read. I think I hear the sound of both hands clapping.

FROM FORTY-EIGHT GATES

5 KYOGEN'S MAN UP A TREE

Who is it that asks
a man holding by clenched teeth
to a branch reaching
out over a precipice
What is the meaning of life?

Let him eat his words.
Let the silence of fungi
beneath the gnarled oaks
of the wood put him to shame.
Let him find his own answer.

8 THE WHEELMAKER

The car does not move.
Someone has taken the wheels,
the axles also.
The car is perfectly still.
The steering wheel does not steer.

Free of intention
I sit in the driving seat.
I'm going nowhere.
Not a speck on the windscreen
clouds my view of what happens.

16 THE SOUND OF A BELL

The sound of a bell.
Does it travel towards you?
Does your ear grasp it
at source? How do you know it

for the bell-sound that it is?

And now the bell sounds
why break off meditation,
wrapping your mind up
in seven awarenesses
to travel the big wide world?

34 MIND IS NOT THE BUDDHA; REASON IS NOT THE WAY

The language of *not*
bars the way, closing two gates.
If I were a cat
I could squeeze my way through them
but these whiskers are human.

Then what beyond mind?
And what beyond reason?
Mindfulness beckons
one way, and love the other.
I'll pass through these, if I can.

46 GO ON FROM THE TOP OF THE POLE

Bamboo mind, nourished
for a hundred years; what, for
the next ten thousand?
Write the next verse, and the next.
How should death interrupt you?

At the end of all
return to the beginning
with a kinder heart;
sit without fear in silence
forgetting all you have learned.

5: Conjectural Musik

THE GOHORRY DOUBLE

John Greening

A few years ago I received the most thoughtful of birthday presents from the editor of this volume. Knowing my love of music, Stuart had suspected that I would enjoy John Gohorry's latest Bach-themed 'magnum opus'. With most writers that expression is just a playful avoidance mechanism when we don't know what else to say about their latest book; with John (and he was John rather than Don to me) it was quite a different matter. Some of his books were huge. This one wasn't on the scale of other Late Gohorry. Nevertheless it was no conventional slim volume. More like a magazine to look at, but 'handbound in Belfast at the Winepress' ('Since before 1632 the Greig sept of the MacGregor Clan has been printing and binding books') by Lapwing Publications ('a bird, in Irish lore … indicative of hope') and set in a quaint-looking Aldine 721 BT, its 75 pages seemed to comprise just two poems, along with innumerable footnotes and endnotes. Even the title required a deep breath: *Impromptus for George Erdmann, a Bildungsgedicht in eighteen episodes & The Good Samaritan, a libretto for a conjectural Abendmusik in five parts*.

In fact, I had already seen some extracts from the Erdmann poem because it came out the year I was compiling an anthology with a similarly long-winded title: *Accompanied Voices: Poets on Composers from Thomas Tallis to Arvo Pärt*. I had earmarked one of John's lighter poems for the section on Percy Grainger and hoped to use his 'A *fiat* for Joseph Haydn' too, but I knew he was likely to have other musical pieces so we were in email contact. When I eventually told him I would like one of the new extracts he had sent me to use in my J.S. Bach section, he wrote back expressing his delight and adding that in the interim the work had 'gone through various drafts' (time had passed because funding for my anthology had been a nightmare) and he wanted to change the title, send an update, add some more footnotes…

That John so loved annotation says something about the sheer breadth of his interests and the unapologetically recondite nature of his poetic subject matter. There was always something Poundian about his productivity, but he was concerned and considerate enough to want to help his readers along – something that EP couldn't have cared less about. In fact, John's notes are not strictly necessary for most of the time, because the music of his lines carries us, but I think he just enjoyed preparing them. I had the impression too that he relished revising. But as it happened, the new version he sent me I simply didn't respond to with such enthusiasm, so he very generously allowed me to use that *Ur-text* in *Accompanied Voices* (he notes the fact with scholarly fastidiousness on the very first page of the Lapwing edition). I don't think many poets would have been so obliging. In his emails, John also gave me some background to the book and the reasons for its complicated title, explaining how it was for a postgraduate music student who was composing the music for it for her Ph.D:

> It's a long saga, but for the sake of the probabilities I needed to have Bach involved in an ordinary Abendmusik while in Lübeck, and in order to be able to frame what he might want to say about his involvement in this in the medium of his impromptus to Erdmann, I felt I had to compose and apportion the various episodes of a possible Biblical narrative first. So I've written a libretto for the story of *The Good Samaritan*, with verbal indications of what kind of music would come where. I was then able to have Bach refer to, and reflect on, his experience of it – as a player, as a composer, and as a human being (not that these things are separate).
>
> After I went to a performance of *The Messiah* at Christmas 2012, it occurred to me that if my libretto were condensed (slightly) and if music could be found for it, it would make a terrific Cantata. I emailed various university music departments, and now here I am, with a realistic expectation of the thing being ready for some sort of performance late next year.
>
> Anyway, the libretto is an integral part of the book, hence the title.

Whether that performance actually happened, I can't remember. I fancy it did. Alas, the launch of my music anthology didn't, so we never had a chance to hear John read the lines I chose.

The story he tells in the 2015 publication is a compelling one, of course: how Bach set out from Armstadt in mid-October 1705 to walk the 250 miles to Lübeck in order to hear Buxtehude play the organ. John's poem joins a long procession of walking poems, from Chaucer's Canterbury pilgrims to Wordsworth on the Duddon right up to Simon Armitage's coastal explorations and Alice Oswald beside the Dart. He explains in the introduction how the project took root in 2005/6 with a single short poem which was accepted for *Poetry Review*, and made him realise that the pilgrimage was 'somewhat analagous to the journeys of self-discovery that attract many young people in their late teens today to undertake voluntary service at home or overseas'. But he couldn't see a way to develop this and meanwhile 'turned to other projects' – chiefly two other long poems, *Samuel Johnson's Amber* (Shoestring, 2010) and *The Age of Saturn* (Shoestring, 2015) which he had been labouring on for three decades. What interested him, he explains, was 'setting up parallel and reflecting interactions between two contrasting – in fact antithetical – yet complementary characters.' In the first book it was Johnson and the fictitious Malachi (Malarkey) Macpherson; in the second, Hölderlin and Goya. What he lacked for the Bach story was an equivalent pairing since the composer 'had no constant companion on the journey'. It wasn't until 2010/11 that he realised that George Erdmann might offer the solution: he was a school friend of Bach's, and there was just enough evidence to make it 'entirely reasonable' (and luckily not too much to make it improbable) that Bach could have kept his friend updated by letter during his Lübeck adventure. Those letters turned to what John called – in an anachronistic Schubertian touch – 'impromptus', a writing-out of Bach's ideas for his friend to see when they met, a kind of archive, moulded as far as possible into the possible calendar of the composer's actual journey. The *Abendmusik* text, the libretto (the second poem in the book), emerged in 2014 to be set by composer Anna Krause – now Anna Albinson. John explains in the introduction that Bach probably arrived in Lübeck just as rehearsals for the *Abendmusiken* began at the end of October.

Copies of John's long poems are not always easy to come by, but they are well worth reading, and not as forbidding as their presentation makes them seem. Invariably they are crafted with taste and originality. The long informal line he chose for the 'impromptus' (a species of hexameter — i.e. with six beats) is very effective indeed, managing to retain something conversational while sounding sufficiently elevated. Here is the opening of Section X, only omitting three footnotes which (i) explain that the reference to Justitia alludes to Erdmann's study of jurisprudence, (ii) give the precise dates of the performances alluded to, and (iii) tell us that Tesdorpf was a wine importer and guild member:

11 p.m. Wednesday 23 December 1705, at the Schafferey, Lübeck

Espressivo assai

It's almost Christmas, George, and whether you spend it
    back home
in Ohrdruf or further afield, I send you my warmest greetings.
I hope that Justitia, weighing you in her scales, looks with pride
on her most diligent student, and that in her name Providence
showers you now and in future with rewards for good service.
I could wish the same for myself because here a large grey cat
has walked into the Altmarkt and sent all the pigeons flying.
The weeks since I last wrote opened auspiciously, as Cecilia
and I enjoyed two conversations of understanding, venturing
each time forward a little further over ground that proved
firmer with every exchange, until in the unsearchable space
that some represent as a garden, and others a paved colonnade
and which all know is neither heart nor head but the hinterland
in which each is the other, each heard the other as counterpoint
on the keyboard of the affections. The last two remaining parts
of *The Good Samaritan* have been rehearsed and performed
to the delight and illumination of all, an act of compassion
invoked with such depth of feeling that Patron Tesdorpf, come

down from his seat in the choir, pronounced it *beautifully drawn and delivered...*

For reasons explained in the copious end-notes, *The Good Samaritan,* which makes up the second part of the 2015 book, is told largely in ballad metre, or perhaps we should think of it as hymn metre – a challenge to the composer, one imagines, since strophic songs can be monotonous. Bach showed how it can be done successfully in his chorales, although John's verses smack more of Schubert's Wilhelm Müller or Schumann's Heine. Naturally, he carries it all off with great aplomb as here at the opening of Part III:

Sunday 6 December (*sic*) (Advent II)

[Organ prelude]

1

Nuntius (Tenor)
An injured man lies in the road,
robbed, wounded, left for dead;
his wallet, suitcase, cloak are gone;
the ruthless thieves have fled.

Good folk, on errands bent, pass by,
and do not offer aid;
their business is important and
they must not be delayed.

Others along life's dusty track
in search of pleasure speed;
they pass by on the other side,
indifferent to his need.

Still others, born to better things
view suffering with distaste;
they do not wish to soil their hands
and scuttle by in haste.

I raise my eyes and scrutinise
this faithful congregation;
which of us turns aside to be
an injured man's salvation?

[Orchestra]

The fast-moving narrative of the libretto with its brisk clichés, old-style inversions and simple rhymes makes a nice contrast with the more ponderous unrhymed Erdmann story, although it does cry out for performance and loses a great deal on the page, where it can feel more like doggerel. But it is very craftsmanlike doggerel, with bold touches such as the heavy opening spondee on 'robbed, wounded' where one might expect an iamb. The semi-colons too are an indication of the poet's concern for precise rendition. Both here and in the eighteen impromptus, the punctuation and syntax, the poetry's architecture, the placing of motifs, the attention to sound all suggest a profoundly musical instinct at work.

I wish that I had found the time to sit down with John and talk about music, to tell him that the name Lübeck was an important one to me since my father had been there at the end of the war and we even had an old Pye 'Golden Guinea' LP of Bach being played by Michael Schneider on the very organ Bach had gone to hear. Or indeed to talk with him about our shared love of Hölderlin, subject of that earlier long poem. Alas, it never happened. But I honour his extraordinary work, as I do the memory of a lovely man and remarkable poet.

FROM HÖLDERLIN AT THE PIANO

IN CONTRARY MOTION

The hands sweep notes from the keyboard like leaves from a lawn,
the swish and brush of their currents composing a slow narrative
of attenuation in which the synchronised words of farewell
are uttered in what grow to intervals of one and more octaves,
an estrangement of voices that although distance between them
increases lose no resonance as they travel one pace at a time
towards opposite ends of the platform. He thinks of them

as soldiers on ceremonial duty outside the Royal Palace
if Ludwigsburg, or in this latter age Rosenstein,
who stand side by side at the centre, facing the front,
then stamping their feet, turn their backs on each other
and marching in step, stride with deliberate slowness,
each to his own set of railings at the extremity
some two hundred metres away, halt, stamp and turn

as both hands now with a flourish acknowledge their limit
at the far ends of the keyboard, and with an about turn
start the journey towards reunion. He thinks of himself
as the left hand, working his way up out of travail,
and his right the beloved, stepping gracefully down
from her dwelling among the stars into a middle ground
where they might meet and embrace; the conceit urges him

towards an *accelerando* that he reproves in the same instant
because hope is a delusion and the laws of the universe
sentence those that break ranks to despair. The hands move
towards and towards in a tempo that does not vary; the mind
that expresses itself through them enforces a discipline
strict in every particular. At the centre again they turn,
part, sweep notes from the keyboard like leaves from a lawn.

AN IMPROMPTU

It's a cold winter's morning and the carpenter's offcuts
that lie in the grate have not taken. The fire's had its chance
and he might attend to it later, but you can't go running about
at the beck and call of every failed enterprise, and at the moment
the most important thing is to start playing. So he puts on
his black winter greatcoat and thermal fingerless gloves
and with only himself for audience takes his seat at the piano.

He begins, and with eyes closed plays in a minor key only,
since it's a Thursday and the Neckar is frozen solid. Notes
drop from his hands like birds from a dead sky, in perfect accord
with the cold in his heart. The piano is the black pediment
of a collapsed mausoleum, the keyboard an icebound river
where barges, in twos and threes, fret at their moorings.
An E flat, when he clambers aboard it, resonates with the griefs

of a lifetime of servitude; a soft A downstream is so plangent
it brings a lump to his throat. When it snows on the keyboard
sound tumbles in thick flakes and the room fills with the mauve
light of a sky that encloses; his hands reach out over powdery
scales for the right notes, yet reaching towards and away down
the slippery keyboard leave no prints. The morning moves on
and behind him the girl of the house has come in without fuss

and coaxed fire from the hearth. She stands and listens until
a phrase in the left hand intrigues him, and leaves as he plays it
over and over again. The chill of the room lifts and the barges
begin to jostle. The keyboard unfreezes, and for a moment
he glimpses the major, imagines taking his coat off, but the fire
will have gone out by evening and it's better to keep playing
the way you began with this rigmarole of the world going on.

6: Hear-no-Good, See-no-Good, Tell-you-no-Lies

AMONG THE YAHOOS

Stuart Henson

Asked whether it was possible to write poetry without political engagement—in a podcast in 2019—John Gohorry's reply was unequivocal: 'I don't think there's any alternative,' he says. 'Being a poet is indistinguishable from engaging with what's out there.'[*] The question was part of a discussion that focused, inevitably at that time, on Brexit and John's new book *Squeak, Budgie!* but the response is typical of the man I knew. His views were 'robust'—not in the clichéd political use of the word but in the sense of being vigorous, sincere, courageously held. His stance was never partisan in a tub-thumping radical way. More Swiftian, I'd say—more ironic and nuanced. Indeed, the loss of nuance in current political and social discourse was one of John's genuine regrets. He expresses it in a poem he reads for the podcast which begins, 'La Nuance est morte' and continues, in his English translation, 'Wrap up her corpse in a shroud made of certainties…' The action of writing bilingually (as he did in the collection *Adagios en Ré*) was itself a political statement. He was, as will be evident elsewhere in this volume, a passionate Europhile.

With his love of balance and formal dexterity, he was also something of an Augustan, though for *Squeak, Budgie!* he was pleased to look to an earlier, equally ruthless, age for his model. The text, which began as a series of Facebook postings, was published by Smokestack shortly before our final departure from the European Union. 'Patriotism has been hijacked by people who have a very narrow concept of what patriotism is,' he observes. He was joking when he said he hoped to reach 'a hundred million followers' on Facebook, but he did want *Squeak, Budgie!* to be sufficiently noticed 'to make a difference'. What follows is the review I wrote at the time for *London Grip:*

'Pipsqueak, the eponymous Budgie, has distinguished antecedents. His forebears can be found among the Budgerigars

[*] https://podcasts.apple.com/gb/podcast/breaking-lines/id1458392702?i=1000445327412

and the polyglot Parrot of John Gohorry's first book *A Voyage Round the Moon*:

> Psittacus, preening himself on his high perch,
> is a fine fellow for feathers and for *declensio verbi*;
> for *quis est puer pulcher vel pulchrior*, search
> *hic et ubique*, none has his quality.

His mother's lineage can be traced back to John Skelton's 16th Century satire *Speke Parrot*. Indeed, Skelton's *Peerless Papagay* puts in a guest appearance at the end of the present book to join with Pipsqueak in a valedictory lament for a more liberal and enlightened age. Young Pipsqueak (he's young in spirit at least) is not inclined to withdraw to an ivory-tower, or hide his light under a cage-cloth. He's out there mixing it with the politicians and pundits to try to make sense of the shambles that goes under the joyless name of *Brexit*. His *modus operandi* is, naturally enough, satire—and he's not afraid of getting his beak dirty.

Following Pipsqueak is better than watching Peston or Andrew Marr, and Pipsqueak isn't bound in the way that journalists are to be even-handed. ('Pipsqueak is a working bird, a listener, an *Inside Ear*') His *magnum opus* takes us, from November 2016 through to May of this year, encompassing the rise of Trump, the triggering of Article 50, the Windrush scandal and the World Cup along the way. The poem's constructed in a series of parts or chapters— Parliament must have a Meaningful Vote, Pre-Eurosummit manouvres, Making Fudge at Chequers—cast in a lively and irreverent rime royal:

> *Pipsqueak*'s tapestry, unfinished, many splendoured and various,
> depicts all these episodes, people, places and things;
> in these times of the good, of the bad, the absurd, the nefarious,
> he beavers away to record what our history brings.
> Shall we regain on the roundabouts half what we lose on
>   the swings?
> Can *Pipsqueak* bring daylight into a darkened room
> and his small querulous voice somehow dispel the gloom?

It's a relief to have such a clear sighted commentary—that

engages with the political at a sophisticated level yet leavens its message with humanity and self-mockery.

> He'll bring more light than heat to our selfish, retributive age
> for if *Pipsqueak* can't teach man respect for his fellow man
> in these mischievous times, tell me, what birdbrain can?

Each part is rounded with a song—pop, folk, rap, a song for Europe—and these are punctuated, medieval-style, with Latin choruses. (Pipsqueak studied those endangered subjects modern languages and Latin at school, and he puts his scholarship to excellent use.) The burden of these songs is: 'Step into other people's shoes / and walk along the street; / confound your prejudicial views; / see if perspectives meet. // *In calceis aliorum mundum per oculos aliorum videre potes.*'

That's not to say that Gohorry's satire is in any way namby-pamby when it comes to 'calling-out' the villains of the piece. When Dominic Raab gives Michel Barnier a copy of *The Hedgehog and the Fox*, '*Pipsqueak* has read Berlin's essay, and smelling a rat, / sees how easy it is to turn all *Raab* implies on its head, / reading *EU* as fox and *UK* as hedgehog instead.'

> Like the hedgehog we're stuck in pursuit of a single end,
> curled up in our insular ball, unprepared to rethink;
> lacking lateral thought, *Hedgehog Britain*'s unable to bend,
> but trundles its way ever closer towards the brink.
> Bigots, liars and shysters throw all bar the kitchen sink
> in the wake of an ill-judged and badly-flawed referendum
> and no-one is left with the will, strength and means to upendum.

Among the aforementioned, we encounter *Bullingdon Boris, Spreadsheet Phil* and the unyielding *Cousin Arlene*. One of the most acidic of the songs, to the tune of 'Good-night Irene', resounds with the chorus (*Nunc omnes in commune*) '*Arlene*, squeeze tight etc. ... They need your votes tonight.' The poet's responsibility is to hold as t'were a mirror up to nature, and Pipsqueak's '*speculum*'s programmed with up-to-date *Squeak Recognition*'.

What the mirror reveals would make many budgies despair
but *Pipsqueak*'s resourceful, resilient, hard as nails,
and *Mischief* must go to the wall where his satire prevails.

So this is neither a soft-centred piece of rhyming doggerel—we've heard enough of those recently on trailers for sporting events and after national disasters—nor a left-wing diatribe. The uncomfortable *Jezza*, though by and large admired, comes under the equal scrutiny of the budgie's beady eye. It's rather a plea for maturity, compassion and generosity in public life. Pipsqueak paces his cage and asks 'what *Prime-Ministers* know / of the angst-ridden lives of the people they represent'. Unsurprisingly, it's a stance that gets him into trouble, with the Home Office, and at the conclusion he finds himself facing deportation by 'a country reclaiming control of its national borders.' Still, his avian brethren flock down to his party, and a plea of mitigation is entered by Skelton's Macaw, hoping that

> *...whoever examines the picture that Squeak, Budgie! paints*
> *will have no truck with political gobbledegook;*
> *they'll come forward in droves to get Pipsqueak the Brave off the hook*
> *and their children, years later, will turn to its pages in search*
> *of the truths and home-truths delivered from Pipsqueak's perch.*

We have, as John Gohorry reminds us finally, in his own voice, to live with our choices. In *Squeak, Budgie!* he's contributed a courageous and timely book to the public debate. Buy it. Read it. Share it. Send it to your MP. Before it's too late.'

Sadly, the pleas of the budgie went largely unheard, and Pipsqueak was too well-mannered to offer any subsequent I-told-you-so's.

But *Squeak, Budgie!* is by no means a one-off foray into the rough-and-tumble of the political. John's engagement with social issues can be seen in the poem 'Boat People' from *A Voyage round the Moon* (1985) which he also reads in the *Breaking Lines* podcast, and where his frustration with the complacency of our representatives in the eighties chimes presciently with our current concerns about the welfare of migrants:

Adrift at sea in the crowded, stinking hulks
you cursed the saviour crook whose filthy berth
bred cholera, exposure, famine, death.
Was there no place for you on the wide Earth?
...

Prisoners of temporising, pious lies
your children died marooned on poisoned shores
or starved in cardboard huddled shanty towns
while politicians bickered over laws.
...

Now that you are among us, know we are
if not the best, the best that you could find;
selfishly just, and meanly generous,
teach us the common virtues of mankind.

It's interesting, and not untypical, that at the end of the poem the roles of benefactor and recipient are reversed. The oxymorons of the penultimate line hit hard, and where the cap of shame fits, we have to wear it.

The same concern for the welfare of the dispossessed can be seen in the overtly social pieces John Gohorry contributed to the *London Progressive Journal*[*] in the years between 2014 and 2020. The last of these, posted in May 2020, brings us clear-eyed into the new world of Covid 19 and the Government's pleas for us to pull together in the face of the healthcare crisis the virus engendered. Its title refers to the regular television addresses that were part of the landscape of the pandemic.

BRIEFINGS

From the chimneys of bar charts
lives vanish in puffs of smoke.

---

[*] https://londonprogressivejournal.com/?s=john+gohorry

>Ministers furnish statistics
>that point to their competence;
>
>they praise, reassure, counsel,
>threaten, instruct, do some good.
>
>From their management platforms
>they thank us, the British people,
>
>for our guts, our compliance.
>We are tough, proud, courageous,
>
>we have battled it all before,
>we have never surrendered.
>
>I remember Sir Geoffrey's players
>sent in to open the batting
>
>with kit their own captain let spoil
>through neglect or austerity.
>
>Have we learned nothing yet?
>Can government never change?
>
>The graph of our suffering
>is the graph of my indignation.

Once again, it's typical that John Gohorry is prepared to acknowledge that even incompetent ministers will, on occasion, manage to 'do some good'. But he's under no illusions about the calculation of the Churchill allusions, the jollying-along from a Prime Minister for whom political expediency is the prime concern. This is a poem shaped around the images of the stats introduced so often with the chilling 'Next slide, please.' The 'chimneys' of the bar-charts cast long historical shadows. The cry of indignation in the closing sentence is Blake's cry—and the cry of our time.

One of the print journals that consistently supported John's work was *Stand*—founded by John Silkin in the fifties to 'stand against injustice and oppression'—and fittingly it was the site of one of his last publications. A Gulliver sequence appeared in *Stand 19/1* in early 2021. It serves, in a way, as a coda to *Squeak, Budgie!* and suggests that he'd found a new hero to impersonate in the 'post-truth' era. I've included all three poems here for that reason. John Gohorry was himself incapable of speaking what the houyhnhnms call *the thing that was not*. And like the houyhnhnms we could wish he was still here among us, working to dismantle the fences that set us apart.

ROUGUE HOUYHNHNM

He was weary of grass and oats,
bored stiff on his diet
of truth, mare's milk and reason.

On the far side of the field
he could pick out the Yahoo crops
that they swore threatened no harm;

there was borage, box privet, ragwort,
the promise of leadership,
setting the country to rights.

Those blues and golds tempted him;
should he cross to the shady side
and swallow *the thing that was not*,

the next Houyhnhnm Assembly
would be his for the taking.
What was there to hold him back?

He'd deny having ventured,
having uttered one word of untruth,
challenged the lie of the land.

GARAFE IN THE HOUYHNHNMS' ASSEMBLY

Look at you, he declared.
Call yourselves horses?
When did you ever work?

All you ever did was dressage.
Prancing about, living the high life.
Best quality stables, hay too,

and plenty of it. Never been short,
have you? Never been hungry.
And all at the taxpayer's expense.

You should all be sent home,
back to the places you came from;
back to work, earning a living.

His speech was translated
into their two working languages;
the horses listened, untroubled,

though faintly embarrassed;
they were used to the discourtesies
he masked as plain speaking.

GULLIVER AMONG THE HOUYHNHNMS

When the fields were fenced off, the Houyhnhnms
heard bands playing, patriot shouts; the land, it was said,
would return to its rightful owners.

Flags flew from accustomed poles and were waved
by those who erected fences; the iron wheels
of steam engines pounded the streets in triumph.

But investment went elsewhere. Centres of learning
saw their horizons shrink; there was talk everywhere
of rupture, of secession. New managers were appointed

to govern the farms, on which the weeds flourished
—nightshade and prejudice, ragwort. The price of grass
as it festered in airless barns went through the roof.

The hospitals promised would not now materialise.
Gulliver's wound would not heal. He'd remain
with the Houyhnhnms, work to dismantle fences.

THE PUBLIC POET

Merryn Williams

My last contact with John Gohorry was on Facebook just three days before he died, and there was no hint then that anything was wrong. He had been discussing a recent programme on Pope which I'd also watched, and although I had always thought Pope boring, that programme made me think again. The old man was a moral poet as well as a very skilful one. He worked hard at his verses, he did not seek a patron; in an age of religious persecution he argued for tolerance and decent behaviour. This is how John celebrated him in a superb parody from 2020:

AUGUSTAN

(for Louis Bailey)

I talked today with Alexander Pope,
Enquired how I might leave my barren Slope
And from Parnassus' Foothills, like him, rise
To where Invention's Beacon fills the Skies,
Shedding such glorious Light on all our Days
First to arouse, and after to amaze.
'First follow Nature,' the great Man replied,
'Then take, like Virgil, Homer as your Guide.
Let Reason lead the way to Eminence,
And Rhetoric keep Step with Common Sense.
With nice Decorum shrewdly start to climb,
And banish mere Sensation from each Rhyme.
Eschew the Low, the Vulgar spawned in Dust,
From your Muse learn to celebrate what's just.
With ceaseless Labour polish every Line;
Correct, discard, re-work, revise, refine,
Until each Word as smoothly seems to flow
As Rivers through their rocky Channels go

With piping Treble, solemn Bass profound,
And Diapason closing up the Sound.
Observe these Precepts; keep them in your Heart;
With Diligence and Patience serve your Art;
And you may find, in Years if not in Weeks,
Footsore and weary, you approach the Peaks;
You seize each Hour; you have no Time to waste;
You glimpse at last the Summit of Good Taste,
And fall upon your Knees, as fall you ought,
To thank your Muse for all the Gifts she brought.
Push upward; end one Verse; begin the next,
And finally, like me, become your Text;
My Blessings, Poet of a later Age,
Inform your Thought and permeate your Page.'

He halted, doffed his Wig, and then and there
Dissolved, as Cloud dissolves, into thin Air.

John looked much younger than his age; it's hard to believe that he has gone, and so fast.

But I would like to celebrate him as a public poet, of whom there are not very many worth celebrating. Consider poets from the past running after patrons, Horace writing odes to Augustus Caesar, Shakespeare grossly flattering the Earl of Southampton, Tennyson kowtowing to Queen Victoria, and all those talentless Laureates. How I hated reading *Absalom and Achitophel* in the sixth form with a right wing teacher! It was written to celebrate Charles the Second, and was about an obscure political crisis which in the end came to nothing, and was full of allusions to long-forgotten men, but the teacher made sure that we got the main point:

> For colleges on bounteous kings depend
> And never rebel was to arts a friend.

Of course, that isn't true today. Poets do not now expect to be paid by the state and are a stroppy and nonconformist lot, on the whole. But they usually prefer to write about private matters; there are thought to be only two great subjects, love and death.

Can public events also inspire good poetry? They can, perhaps more often than we think. There was 'Son of the Red Judge' on the death of Llewellyn, Marvell's Horatian Ode on the execution of Charles I, Hardy's 'Convergence of the Twain' on the loss of the *Titanic*. The two world wars invaded people's private lives and inspired a lot of bad, and some marvellous poetry. Television brought a whole new dimension to human experience, and I've seen a great deal of dreadful doggerel, and just a few good pieces, about the Twin Towers.

John's great subject in his later years was Brexit. He was passionate about the folly of rejecting Europe, sickened by the gutter press's mindless nationalism, and refused to be reconciled to the referendum result. He did not wait to find an editor but posted stanzas on Facebook as they were written, every few weeks for over two years from November 2016. They were published by Smokestack Books in 2019 under the title of *Squeak, Budgie!* and are a bitter, hilarious, up-to-the-minute response to 'Brexit, Trump, the refugee crisis, the rise of neo-Fascism, international crises, a royal wedding, a World Cup, the Chequers agreement, cabinet resignations, the Windrush scandal and the implosion of the Tory party' (I quote from the blurb). Like Skelton and Pope, he thought that satire was not just about being funny but had a noble purpose:

> we stripped the mask off hypocrisy, ridiculed the absurd,
> exposed government folly, taught selfishness charity,
> and awoke what was decent in erring humanity.

I re-read 'Cross-Channel traffic is a matter of concern', first published in January 2019, in the week, nearly three years later, when another boat packed full of refugees went down. That will go on being relevant. But just because Budgie was so up-to-the-minute he is now dated, and if there is a centenary edition of his book it will need more footnotes than *Absalom and Achitophel*.

Yet certain poems about great events are fine enough to stand alone. Donald Trump and his graceless manner of leaving office are, unfortunately, part of history, and John's 'His Doubt Tree' is a splendid work which deserves to go into any collection of political poetry:

HIS DOUBT TREE

> Decent losers are more important for the functioning of a democracy than radiant winners.
> (Heiko Maas, German Foreign Minister, 6 November 2020)

'If the election is fair,' his spokeswoman said,
'we'll accept the result.' She laid no stress on 'If',
but she'd prepared the ground for his Doubt Tree.

When a white officer's knee squeezed the life
from a black man face down on the pavement,
he didn't condemn cop brutality; when anger

erupted, his platform was 'Law and Order'
sending troops in to suppress the precincts.
Right-wing vigilantes gave armed backup

but his quarrel wasn't with them; his targets
were human rights activists, anarchists, antifas
marching to tell the White House 'Black Lives Matter.'

His Doubt Tree took root among cottonwoods.
Through fake soil it burrowed and spread. Unmasked,
he mocked those that wore them while folk died.

Infected, he didn't drink bleach, but cocktails
of Regeneron, and recovered. He was Superman,
stronger than ever, his illness a gift from God.

He knew that a win must be his red certainty,
so he disrupted debate, drowned Blue Rallies
with heckled shouts, Doubt Tree chants, car horns.

Process was corrupt, he alleged. He hustled
his preferred nominee into the Supreme Court,
a judge he believed would buy Doubt Trees.

On E-night, the Blue Vote was surging. His cohorts
battered the courthouse windows, clamouring
'Open the doors, let us in, stop the count!'

But the counting continued. One after another,
institutions called a result that was not his.
He refused to concede, tweeting 'I won – by a lot!'

The result must prove process unfair. His lawyers
launch multiple lawsuits, flimsy, quickly dismissed.
The world scorns the worst kind of loser, a bad one.

He'll walk or be walked from power on the due date
but his Doubt Tree has flowered, and people still
trusting his say-so will nurture their grievances

for another four years at least. What prospect
for healing then, while mischief, misinformation,
the sour fruits of his Doubt Tree, ripen and fall?

This isn't just about a U.S. President's bad behaviour and the terrifying power of demagogues; it's also about a specific time in history, Black Lives Matter, and Covid, and a change of 'leadership of the free world' all clamouring for our attention at once. Like Marvell's poem, also about the fall of a famous man, I like to think that it will still make sense some hundred years from now.

While 2020 rolled on, more and more people were catching, and sometimes dying from Covid. (It's still happening as I write these words in early 2022). Literally thousands of poems about the pandemic got written and I searched out the best of them for a Covid anthology, *Poems for the Year 2020*. John sent me three, 'Briefings', 'Five Stanzas a Day', and 'Pandemic'. I was overwhelmed, and didn't include them, which I now deeply regret. Looking at them again, I see how good they are, how they stress the importance of keeping poetry alive in a dark time and how he skewered the pomposity and incompetence of our elected rulers. Here is the whole of 'Pandemic':

PANDEMIC

Death is two metres away
now, as he always was.

Too close not to notice,
too close for comfort,

he's already at home
in our neighbour's lungs,

the man with the bad cough,
the pick-breath gone viral.

He's the Fatal Fractal
who divides and spreads,

incubates in our mucus,
multiplies, travels on.

Distance preserves us,
the clear Perspex screen

barring breath, barring contact,
his appetite cannot cross,

and the gloved hands
of the compassionate ones,

selfless, masked, unrelenting,
who ventilate and inspire.

John did not die of Covid, but, as he knew, death is still only two metres away. Lives can vanish in a puff of smoke, into thin air. But a life of achievement continues to matter, and we are fortunate that we have still got his poetry.

A SUNSET MEDITATION

The tide rolls and reflections of sunset
float in on the curl of the waves. It's the end
of a summer's day, and I'm here on the beach
to bear witness to transformation. Underfoot
sandhoppers flitter, the prey of small birds
that bustle about the tideline; elsewhere,
the people who came have relinquished
their space to constructions of stone,
driftwood enclosures, small towers crowned
with crab skeletons, shells, drifts of seaweed.

I watch the sun, crimson and scarlet, begin
to conjure its disappearance, dropping down
at the horizon so slowly, it seems, I can't tell
whether movement itself is illusion. The sea,
here, fades in a tranquil expanse that reaches
towards an infinity that remains undisturbed
as the sun thirsts for concealment; the sky,
yellow-mauve minutes ago, shades to purple.
Half submerged now, the sun reaches midpoint
in its parable of extinction, an orange diameter

pared already to segment. I think of the day;
of my days in their tens of thousands, charged
with hope and regret, desire and indifference,
failure, ambition, love, satisfaction, unkindness,
all drowned in their nights and tomorrows
as the fingernail sun now at the world's edge
drowns in eternity. Now it's gone, as it seems
in an instant, a moment of dissolution I saw
with my own eyes, and have lived through. Light
floods the sky in its aftermath, and in its wake,

participant more than witness, I see myself,
feet brushed by sandflies, lit in the backwash
of all my days in the sun, bound for drowning.
Enough then that hunger for spectacle bring me
to meditate and reflect here on the sea's edge
at a time of day when things happen; enough
that tomorrow, come as it may, elsewhere
or returning, I am glad of my life in all colours
—bright-brilliant, dull, sombre, divided as here,
now the sun goes, changed by all that occurs.

THE STOCK EXCHANGE OF IDEAS

David Van-Cauter

On the *Stock Exchange of Ideas*
Originality's failing. Last month the *Index*
of Inspiration closed fifty points down
as *Dullness* continued to gain ground
and *Derivatives* rose to a new high.

Suffering from a dearth of ideas was never an accusation you could level at John Gohorry. Over the course of fifteen years with him at Poetry ID in Letchworth, I witnessed these ideas taking shape, revising and discussing them, until they formed into poems, sequences, pamphlets and sometimes lengthy conceptual books. The double meaning in the title of this, his twelfth collection, is a good summation of how I saw him – he regarded creativity as a shared, collaborative process, which enables us all to communicate in a more meaningful way. The title poem explores this playfully, using a monetary conceit to underline the idea that we only really advance as individuals and as a society by listening to and learning from each other. John always tried to spread his own wisdom, whilst remembering to take on board the views of those around him. These qualities helped to make him an excellent poet – articulate but reflective, loud but willing to listen.

Anyone who experienced John at a poetry reading would remember him – the large voice, the large personality. He never needed a microphone. Often the background to his poems would be longer than the poems themselves, usually because they were part of his latest epic sequence. He loved to embellish his work with details from history and elucidate complicated multi-layered ideas through his remarkable skill with formal verse. Several poems in this collection echo this, but generally it showcases his lighter touch, shorter and with more direct meaning, such as the call for acceptance and willingness to change in 'Other' or the climate crisis in 'A Platform of Words', where he asks:

> What poetry shall we make
> out of gurgle and suffocate?

It's hard to believe that John is gone. Only a few days before his heart attack, we were in a workshop together and he was full of his usual energy and enthusiasm. He was always generous in his feedback, which was derived from his lifelong passion for poetry. His ability to hone language was matched by his intellectual confidence, but he always tried to use this in a way that was helpful, rather than coming across as showy or standoffish. There was a positivity to everything he said, but in his writing he was never afraid to shy away from the darkness. In 'You Sit On The Back Row', we see his anger at the feeling of helplessness when faced with the chaos of the world: the seismic aftershocks of an underground atomic explosion,

> a massacre in a high school,
> starvation, rapes, torture, beheadings

His answer? To suggest that we focus on our 'freedom of thought' and, ultimately, to 'make all the difference you can.' This is only a solution on a personal level, driving away the demons in your head, but inevitably failing to impact on the world stage. In his tribute to Jeremy Corbyn, we see his enthusiasm for the idealist, as he shows how a man putting his head above the parapet, trying to effect real change, is liable to become the target. The press preferred to 'get the man' than to engage with his potentially radical ideas: 'Put on a proper suit... Do up your tie.' The poem expertly cuts down this shallow, bullying line of attack, emphasising the dignity of compassion and humanity over the pointless peripherals. The closing line 'No need to get personal' shines brightly with a barbed ambiguity.

The theme of what constitutes 'personal' in the context of society runs throughout the collection. Sometimes the righteous 'self' appears to be in control, but it seems unaware of the value of compromise or the repercussions of its actions, as in 'After Fo-Yan':

> Bang your fist on the table
> and the universe comes into being.

In 'Letter from Lesbos', he links the historical sense of personal integrity demonstrated by the people of the island, for whom love and acceptance are a part of their identity, with the contemporary crisis of being overwhelmed by migrants escaping war-torn countries. He shows how these cultural values inform their politics, hoping that they might be an example to the people of England, a nation he suggests is less ruled by the instincts of love and more by feelings of distrust and xenophobia. That these views were highlighted, encouraged even, during the Brexit referendum, greatly saddened him. He saw love and understanding as amongst humanity's greatest qualities, and when these were seen wanting, he was unafraid to call it out, asking for less division and more compromise:

> our shames were intolerance,
> pride, whatever withheld love.

As if to reinforce that fundamental change is possible, the imagery of transformation crops up repeatedly. In 'Green', the poet turns into a tree, 'spread into a thousand deltas' as his lifeline stretches to encompass the natural world. It is a strong vision of how the individual intellect can come to terms with the world's complexity, by digging deep into the soil and becoming a part of it. But it begins with a wound – the route is not one that the poet chooses. Instead, he is forced into it through circumstance: pain and necessity. The change that occurs is unexpected but revelatory:

> My heart, once red, is now green, and these notes
> that you think of as words are pure birdsong.

'The Headdress' describes a professor who collects feathers on his daily runs, eventually collecting enough to fashion a hat to wear as he does so. He 'becomes' a bird to escape from his world of academia but discovers that he learns more about himself in the process, 'true happiness' when allowed out of his confines, 'the broad flight of mind above circumstance', taking an oblique path to the truth. A similar process takes place in 'A Sackful of Cloud', where the gift of a cloud is poured into the speaker's left eye. It blurs his reality, but ultimately leads to a new place of understanding. 'Cloud doctors' try to stop it spreading, but he keeps it in check with his other eye, swallowing the mist whilst also seeing through it, utilising its mysteries.

The idea of eyes working differently is also explored in 'Good Eye, Bad Eye'. The bad eye sees the poet as a boy, misbehaving, and he seems to be a personification of regret. The memories are hazy, hard to pin down, but the man clearly wants to let these feelings go and the bad eye won't let him – the rain conjured 'from a neighbour's attic', perhaps tears, perhaps a symbol of renewal. But it leads to a discovery of 'the mind's eye' – a favourite Gohorry image, and a vital conduit in seeing the world in a new way. He ends the poem with a stark truth:

> Time writes
> our infirmities into her notebook in
> the blink of an eye but life's too short
> for complaint or for blame.

Poetry ID will feel very different without John Gohorry, but his spirit has infused the group, and we will continue to be inspired by his tenacious, prolific writing ethic. Even aged 78, he had shown no signs of slowing down, and he still had a lot more poetry to give. He really believed that poetry could be a transformative power. When he was a guest on the *Breaking Lines* podcast in 2019, he said, 'The way I relate to the world, being a poet, is indistinguishable from engaging with what is out there… I do want to make a difference. I hope I can change minds. That might be a complete folly on my part.' He certainly left us a substantial body of excellent work, and I hope that, in time, he will.

THE STOCK EXCHANGE OF IDEAS

On the *Stock Exchange of Ideas*
Originality's failing. Last month the *Index
of Inspiration* closed fifty points down
as *Dullness* continued to gain ground
and *Derivatives* rose to a new high.

Cliché did well, while *Insight*,
Wit, and *Illumination* fell through the floor.
Imitation was bullish. *Tautology*
prospered where *Brexit* meant *Brexit*
while *Greed* took *Charity* to the cleaner's.

The *Intellectual Policy Committee*
today met in emergency session.
It ruled out *Quantitative Easing*
which it said just meant more of the same
and instead proposed *Poetry Playgrounds*

—nationwide, free, and open to all
wanting to write, paint, sing, play an instrument.
In a climate of sharing, *Imagination*
would bring back former prosperity.
The project would make things happen.

THE SPINNEY

Invisible among hazels,
I lost myself in the spinney,
made up a brushwood shelter
while I was growing teeth,
learning to walk, learning balance,
learning to wear shoes.

At some stage, I went missing,
at some stage, the landscape changed.
I made hundreds of sketches,
drew maps, looking for routes
that were paved, not too steep,
safe, after dark, to be found in.

But the spinney was gone, its place
held by library, bus depot, cinema.
Who I was had gone too. In his place
was a man strange to himself
as to you now, recalling the spinney,
the paths he mapped, that went nowhere.

7: Out Of The Fire Room

THE FIRE ROOM

I came to the Fire Room as a young boy;
it was late autumn and I had been walking
beside the canal, watching the coal barges
inching their way through the sheet ice
between Hawkesbury, Sowe Common and Ansty.

My mother, next door, was laying the table;
I found pencil and paper, a desk and a chair
and sat down in the Fire Room, which was not
part of the house, building my small fire.

In my mind's eye, I could see the barge moving,
its black bow nudging the ice, the dolly-butt
frayed at the edges, the world-weary draw-horse
trudging his way over the iron bridge
at the junction, the tow rope, now slack,
now taut, and the bull arms of the man
at the tiller, wrapped in a dozen greatcoats,
who pulled on his pipe, glanced over at me
and said *Afternoon, Snowball*.
All this I wrote down, doubtless in other words,
then closed the door, joining my mother for tea.

Over the years, I have been to the Fire Room
many hundreds of times. It is never the same
from one day to the next, but I have found
it has means of making things visible—windows,
projection screens, microscopes, all kinds of lenses,
autobiographies, newspapers, history books, fables.
There are shelves stacked with dictionaries, word lists,
boxes of tricks labelled *as, since, before, after, if...then,*
a hypocaust of invention from which I have
only to help myself, a flame not extinguished.

I work in the Fire Room most days, tending and dowsing,
alone as I thought, until now, but for a girl
in the flame coloured silks and the red hair
who dances not only for me, and plays the bassoon,
and whose name sometimes is Aurora.

So brightly she burns some days that my words,
incandescent for hours, scorch the paper I write on;
other days I must scrape away at her damp flints
and hope for a spark. I know she has others to see to.

For years there were only we two, but of late
other guests have appeared in the Fire Room—my father,
for instance, spread-eagled on Courtaulds' roof,
his night glasses sweeping the sky for incendiary bombs,
Dante, close behind Virgil, crossing fiery Phlegethon
in the seventh circle of Hell, and a nine year old girl,
stark naked, screaming, smothered in napalm,
running towards the photographer. And only today
the ghost of my mother, come from the room next door;
the young boy I was, telling her my adventures;
and smoking his pipe, the boatman come gliding by
wrapped in a dozen greatcoats, cold as Death.

PATTERN & PURPOSE

John Lane

I met Don Smith in 1961, when we were both 18. We had attended Bablake Grammar School in Coventry without ever getting to know each other, but our first conversation began a friendship that would continue until his untimely death in 2021. I knew him, and still think of him, as Don Smith; but of course he eventually decided to publish his work as John Gohorry. He never revealed his reason; and I never asked him to tell me. Years later, I came across a clue in his introduction to *Exploring Psalmanazar*, when he says, of George Psalmanazar's two different versions of his autobiography, "I felt no necessity to choose between them but instead grounded my poems in whatever elements of either version, and indeed of my own life, offered creative opportunities." When I reflect on two of the major subjects of his verse – his (Don's) past, often his childhood, experiences, and his (John's) resolve to master the craft of versification – I am glad that I afforded my close friend the privacy which his decision deserved. He too has offered us two autobiographies.

I quickly became aware of his love of words, and his passion for their deployment as messengers for his imagination. He showed me a poem; almost certainly not his first, but one which he assured me was of great significance for him. Its title was *Pattern and Purpose*, and it revealed his lifelong conviction that to be human is to seek, and wherever possible find, – and celebrate – meaning in everything that we experience. His poetry reveals a consistent application of this definitive aspect of his work: he invites us to discover significance in what is at first sight trivial as often as he asks us to ponder on what lies behind philosophical or meditative *discourse* (one of his favourite words). That early poem revealed, too, the ease with which he took on subjects as familiar as mortality:

> …and I shall be united with the ash of autumn bonfires
> and decaying leaf mould underneath bare trees.

His youthful words came back to me, with great sadness, as he was laid to rest not far from his home at Letchworth Garden City.

Like the American poet William Stafford, Don wrote at least one poem if not every day then surely most of the days of his life. And he too kept a journal, filling page after page as he recorded everything that he felt was memorable:

Good days, bad days. I enter them in an archive.

I came to expect, in many of his poems, a reference to some past event which he had once described, transformed by what he calls in one of his poems "the labour of versing." So it was for instance, that half a century after telling me about the felling of a great oak tree which he had held in awe as a child, he wrote

Fifty years fallen
Barnacle Oak still the cage
Of my singing heart.

His knowledge of literature was formidable; I often felt that he could remember everything that he read, not least the work of other poets. He often responded, when I reminded him of a few lines from a poem which I admired, by reciting, without so much as a moment's hesitation, a substantial work such as Donne's *A Nocturnal upon S. Lucie's Day* or a couple of Shakespeare's sonnets. And of course his own work frequently presented a journey for the reader, part factual, part imaginative, into part of the life story of a historical figure. *Samuel Johnson's Amber* and *Impromptus for George Erdmann* fall into this category; and the research which he undertook for works such as these was formidable. He tells us that he laboured from 2011 to 2014 to produce an account of Bach's 250 mile journey from Arnstadt to Lübeck, in 1705. John chose to imagine an account by Bach of his journey, in the form of letters written to his friend Erdmann. With astonishing attention to detail – and plausibility – he explains how he worked out the likely stopping places, and (because Bach walked the entire way) when he would likely have reached each of them. A wonderful example of his diligence – and his imaginative resolve – is revealed when we read, in his introduction, that the first six impromptus bridge the last stretch of Bach's journey and his arrival in Lübeck: "which I presume to have been on the evening of Saturday 31st October."

Much of John's poetry, unlike those collections which deal at great length with such historical material, is more immediately personal, and I shall turn to this soon. But I want to mention a rather tantalising component of his engagement with the likes of Bach, Dr Johnson, Goya and other remarkable individuals. I once asked him if his enthusiasm for delving into the lives of such long departed people was a way of producing work which kept his own, personal experiences out of the picture. He told me that, on the contrary, he wove many of them into his narratives. Some were accessible in some way to the reader – for instance, in *Samuel Johnson's Amber*, p51, we read "In an oblique light in the British Museum reading room, *The Countess of Pembroke's Arcadia* is writing Sir Philip Sidney at an untidy workstation crowded with drafts." On the back cover of the book, we are told that (as Don Smith) his M.Phil dissertation subject was *Sources and Style of Sidney's Arcadia*. I can also confirm that he worked on it at… the British Museum reading room. He often, however, refers to incidents or experiences which only those who shared them – friends, members of his family, colleagues – could reasonably be expected to recognise. I was made all too aware of this part of his creative drive when I mistakenly suggested that one of his works – *A Life of Merlin* – was surely an exception. He pointed out, firstly, that the lines

> Like a boy standing arms outstretched in a summer garden
> who closes his eyes tight and imagines the admirals landing

were in fact a reference to his own childhood experience of butterflies in Coventry. Then he said something that drove home to me his love of learning – and mischievous obscurity. He generously dedicated *A Life of Merlin* to me, and insisted that it contained a reference to our having camped in the Forest of Fontainebleau in the year that we met. I failed to find one. Then I (who have no Latin) discovered that his dedication in the

Bullnettle Press edition – *et fugit siluas uult uideri* – he who flees the woods and wants to be seen – was a typically ingenious reference to the fact that we had fled the forest after a thunderstorm, at my suggestion, and recommenced hitchhiking – hoping, as we thumbed for a lift, to be spotted by a motorist. Such was John Gohorry's love of words, and the many ways in which he loved the way that they can have, or partly hide, meaning. I think that he saw life itself as a journey that unlocked words; after we cycled, with our wives, on the Isle de Ré, he later wrote

> What they notice, they notice,
> riding unhampered
> the road of the five senses,
> the long, green coast of their lives.

Poets, of course, have the right to alter or rearrange facts in the interest of greater truths. He reminds us of this in his poem, called, simply, *Poet,* which appeared on his website:

> dreamer; explorer; wallgazer; fabulist
> …refiner of what first came
> to hand or to mind;

I had a thought-provoking encounter with the fecundity of his poetic licence when I read his prize-winning poem *Lost*. We had spent an idyllic few days in 1963 camping on the banks of the river Cherwell near Kings Sutton. We collected mushrooms from a nearby field and cooked and ate them with relish, but largely survived on apples from an abandoned orchard. We read books, wrote poems, discussed them, and I fished in the river, catching a few tiddlers which we returned to the water. About forty years later, John took these and other details of our adventure and wrote a wonderful and haunting account of…what we had, and had not, experienced. Finding potatoes, catching rabbits, knife throwing, cooking fish, swimming in the cold water of the river: I never of course suggested to John that these and other parts of his poem had not actually taken place. Because when I read, and reread, *Lost* I am taken, as if by magic, to the tranquil, shared fantasy of a kind of Arcadia which we discovered and talked about as early evening mist began to settle over the river. John ends his poem with a lament:

> Home from work, forty years later, I search my house
> for the knife as I search for the old days.
> ...if I look forever, I know I won't find it.

Well, the knife, and our old days, are there in that verse. They are every bit as real as life itself. And I'm sure that if I had ever chosen to query his story of our waterside exploits, he would have laughed. And then reminded me of lines from two other poems: First *Masterminds*:

> Is knowledge merely recollection of the facts?

And then *The Truth About the Past*:

> We listened to one another, and sat up straight,
> told the truth always, did not exaggerate

All of John's friends and family, and indeed a good many of those who met him, will have discovered the ingenious ways he had of sharing something that resonated with him when in their company.

In John's last published work – A Coventry Crucible – almost all of the poems deal with his childhood, and many of them have as their subject the memories he had of his brother Peter. His many references to Peter reveal something which we often find in his verse: his conviction that the passage of time magnifies, rather than diminishing, the significance of all that we remember. In the series of poems called *Mound*, he says of this place which he and his brother often visited

> ...We called the Mound
> *Pekin*, because from the summit
> we had a clear view of China.

Then in the third poem he re-affirms the imaginative game of their childhood:

> We called it *Pekin*, which it still is, a place
> where the joy of pretend, share and imagine
>
> fills me seventy years later, hearing again
> its chatter of magpie and thrush, the rustle
>
> of time in its hawthorns, the calls from about
> of young voices that might be our own.

The sources of John's creativity – his love of language, his reverence for the past, his meditative encounter with Zen, his passion for blending personal or historical information with imaginative alchemy – defy analysis. But there is one other possible reason for his early decision to become a poet. Many years back, we were comparing the effect that a stretch of water in Coventry called Wyken Pool had had on our lives. He told me that he and his brother Peter had once been taken by their father for a boat excursion on the pool, and that they had asked him, as he rowed, how deep it was. I have never forgotten what John said next:

> "He told us that no-one had ever succeeded in answering that question, but the likeliest answer was that it was, to all intents and purposes, bottomless."

John laughed as he told me. And I still believe, all these years later, that this wonderful and humorous fatherly flight of fancy was one of the moments in his life that set him on his tireless quest to show how what we imagine is as real as we want it to be.

LOST

'Some things are truly lost...' (Richard Wilbur, *The Mind Reader*)

That summer we were lost to the whole world
but our open-air, camp-fire selves. An orchard
fruited with early damsons, and the fields
were cram-full of potatoes, so it was easy
to live off the land and to supplement
our stolen pickings with rabbits or fish
from the unsupervised backwaters. Hours long
we lay on the ledgering bank, our lines low
while in deep pools where the current circled
bream nudged and tormented us; hours long
we tended our traps by the burrow-holes
and runs in the meadow grass, then as dusk came
made fire with birch twigs to cook what we had caught
and what we had gathered. We watched the late glow
of the embers until the cold stiffened our backs,
then wrapped ourselves in our small tent, and slept.

Between times, we exercised, daydreamed, read,
wrote verses. We made spears from brushwood staves,
and hurled them great distances, read Sophocles,
Hopkins, Jung, wrote philosophical lines
from the collective unconscious, eulogies
of the dappled woods, elegies for felled trees.
Or we lay in the sun, and I did not share thoughts
of a girl that might come riding from nowhere
on a motorbike stolen from helmeted bad boys,
my skinny scarecrow straight out of Baudelaire
lit with cheap rings, and a crown of crow's feathers
tight round her naked brows. The river was cold
where we swam after hunting, the bed's silt soft
and dark underfoot. On the surface, at eye level,
flies danced, circled, drowned in pools of despair.
I had a knife at that time with an eight-inch blade
that curved and then came to a point. The handle

was moulded to fit the palm, and a cross-piece
kept fingers and thumb protected. The knife slept
at my hip in a sheath held safe by a press-stud
looping over the cross-piece, but all day I used it.
The handle stunned fish, the blade sharpened spears,
fencing stakes, pencils, cut string, tyrant knots, withies.
Its point speared food from the fire, from the pans,
the flat of the blade carried flesh, fruit and tubers
to my mouth, past the edge of my hunger. I could send
the knife flying in cartwheels, bury the point
chest-high in a beech board at ten yards, or throw it
time after time, no more than a blade's length outside
your stretched foot, until you could stretch no further.

Home from work, forty years later, I search my house
for the knife as I search my mind for the old days.
It's not in the loft, garage, or cellar, not among
boxes of old manuscripts, wardrobes of old clothes.
If I look for ever, I know I won't find it.

AN ADMIRER OF FRANCIS PONGE REVISITS HOLCOMBE, DEVON

John Gohorry, 28 March 2020

Invited to write a prose-poem inspired by pebbles, I remember what Ponge did, consulting the best dictionaries for a definition of his subject, and skimming his verse off from there. So I look in his *vade mecum* for a suitable definition.

Littré and Beaujean write not merely of *French pebbles*, but of *pebble* in French. The word is *galet*. Having begun my prose-poem in English, and wrapped my tongue by design round a word from a second language, I enter Babel, encountering a third as the two lexicographers trace the word's etymology back to the Celtic *gal*, a stone. The Celts lived in Brittany, where there is an abundance of stone, most notably in the massed rows at Carnac, the numerous megaliths and menhirs of the region, and also the rocks that make navigation off Paimpol, Plouha, and the outlying islands so perilous. In the Parish Church of Notre Dame de Bonne Nouvelle on the Île de Bréhat there are tables inscribed with the names of the many ships that have foundered there – the three masted *Brunette*, the sloops *Marie-Jeanne* and *Ernest et Georges*, the luggers *Gabrielle*, *Jeanne*, and *Jeanne-Marie* to name only those half-dozen. It was the prospect of her returning husband's shipwreck on these fatal rocks that led Dorigen, the faithful wife of the knight Arveragus in Chaucer's *Franklin's Tale*, to risk compromising her honour by promising Aurelius, her young and passionate suitor, that she will become his lover if he can by some means make those rocks disappear, and so make her husband safe. Little does she imagine that her ardent admirer has access to a magician in Orleans who is capable, through powerful incantations (and an exact knowledge of when neap tides occur), of seeming to bring this about, thereby trapping her between – yes – a rock and a hard place. She must either break her promise to the squire or be unfaithful to her husband.

Arveragus returns from his travels, landing safely from his ship. But the Franklin has him insist, as a man of honour, that his wife must keep her promise. The squire, however, is shamed by this and releases her from it. The magician, in his turn, forgives the squire his fee for services provided. Which of the three, asks the Franklin, can claim to be the most honourable man? All our prior certainties about what constitutes honour founder on the rocks of the Franklin's story.

Should you object at this early stage in my poem about pebbles that it has so far been concerned with rocks, I must answer that rock is the ancestor of pebble; they are linked through boulder, as boulder is linked to stone, and as stone is linked through pebble with his remote descendant, sand. The world of the pebble, like the world of rock and of much else besides, is governed by the Law of Erosion, whose chief agent is Time, and Time, the daughter of Truth, uses all her resources of rain, wind and weather not only to rub away rock's jagged spars and rough edges, but also devotes patient aeons to progressively wearing away its bumps, ridges and coruscations, investing her subject with the polish and smoothness that along with diminutive stature are the distinguishing characteristics of the pebble.

Time's work, we remind ourselves, is ceaseless; her supply of elbow-grease is without end, and her labour of polishing and refining is not one of completion, but of transition. The fate of the pebble is, over time, to be reduced to a mere grain of sand, and the fate of this grain of sand is to be joined with those countless billions of grains that Time keeps in her hourglass so she may herself keep track of years spent in the erosion of worlds. Such is the immense importance of the pebble we pick up during our walk along the beach, rinse free of the grains which have stuck to its underside, and after a few moments of inspection and admiration in the palm of the hand, let drop once again to our feet, or with a flick of the wrist, fling casually into the shallows.

My poem is on a smaller scale than Chaucer's and you will discover it less ambitious in terms both of its social setting and its ethical concerns. It is a poem of pebbles, not rocks, and Ponge's lexicographers, in accordance with a professional code that enjoins them neither to a life of ease, nor to the temptations of a short cut, but on the contrary to semantic completeness, furnish a second sense of this word *galet*, namely *'jeu où l'on pousse un palet sur une longue table.'* With a brief call on the lexicographers to ascertain the meaning of *palet – a flat, round piece of stone, iron or copper, that one propels as closely as possible towards a designated target* – I translate myself from the sea-girt chivalric heights of Middle Age Brittany to the picturesque village of Holcombe, in Devon, where at the age of ten, along with my parents and my younger brother, I first saw the sea.

Born in Montpellier in 1899, Ponge moved when he was ten to Caen, in Normandy, but had plenty of time before then to familiarise himself with the beaches of Maguelone, Espiguette, and Sète, where at that time people still wore clothes in public places, and so had the convenience of pockets in which to carry their loose change. Half a century later, residents and holidaymakers in Holcombe are dressed, not undressed, for the seaside. Our family wear shirts, sunhats, and shorts bought at no small expense from a Coventry outfitter which reach to, or to just below, the knee. My mother, small and elegant in her yellow polkadot frock, carries a matching parasol.

My brother and I stand on tiptoe, peer through the smoke-fogged windows of memory into the public bar of The Castle Inn, where brawny men with Popeye tattoos on their arms are wrestling one another over tables spread with dominoes, beermats, torn open packets of Walkers salt and vinegar potato crisps, sheafs of playing cards and loose coins. In one corner, a game of shove-ha'penny is in progress.

It's over fifty years since the old ha'penny, of which there were no fewer than 480 to £1 sterling, was withdrawn from circulation. It had a profile image of our now 94 year-old Queen on one side, and an image of Sir Francis Drake's ship, *The Golden Hind,* and a year date, on the other. The men in the bar have five ha'pennies apiece, and taking turns, they are attempting, with the flat of the hand, to propel their coins up the board until one of them wins by having lodged three coins in each of the nine narrow beds into which the board is horizontally divided, without overlapping any of the dividing lines. Their scores are kept by chalk marks placed at the edge of each bed, one player taking the right-hand side of the board, the other left. There are shouts of encouragement and of disappointment issuing from the bar; periodically, one of the players refreshes himself from a straight glass of beer at the side of the table.

The notion of a flat piece of stone or metal being propelled towards a target is an appropriate metaphor for the composition of a prose poem such as this; the challenge in both cases is to be able to place the projectile at an exact point, without falling short and without overreaching. There is a particular skill in judging the strength and the direction of the shove, and there is skill too in aiming one of the coins so that it will make contact with another, and propel that towards the destined target, perhaps even lodging itself in a scoring position.

My brother and I have looked through the windowpane long enough and it is evident that the game will go on until closing time or beyond, so we turn round and walk down the hill, passing the thatched eaves of Lobster Cottage, carefully crossing the coast road along which occasional cars and buses ply between Teignmouth and Dawlish, and make our way down Smuggler's Lane to the beach.

Memory glances like a skimmed stone off two features of our walk that late summer's afternoon. The first is the adolescent daughter of a family making their way up from the beach. She is fourteen, perhaps fifteen; tall, slender and sunburned, she wears only a small green bikini fastened with cord at the hip which conceals no more than the minimum modesty requires, and accentuates the graceful motion of her long, slim legs, so that coming towards us she appears to be dancing in slow motion rather than walking. She is barefoot, untroubled by such chippings, gravels and small pieces of stone as remain from when the lane was last surfaced. The top of her bikini is no more than two small triangles of fabric held apart at the front by a length of thin brown cord, and drawn in the opposite direction by strands of the same cord running round her ribcage to meet and be tied between her shoulder blades. She moves free of her parents, holding a shrimp net in one hand. She looks me full in the face as they pass; she has confident, steady, even challenging eyes, and I sense the protective stare of her father, which seems also to contain an element of satisfaction at my embarrassment. I look over my shoulder for her, once, twice, as they reach a bend in the lane, where they vanish from sight and remain, as I thought out of mind, until now.

The second appears as we are passing under a bridge that gives access to the beach. In a cavernous echoing space formed of stone and concrete, reeking of brine and seaweed, we are without warning deafened by a loud whistle and a powerful, rhythmic roar. Our hearts in our mouths, we rush through, and looking up, can make out beyond the rise of the sea wall a train heading for Teignmouth, a plume of smoke from the engine streaming back over the fast-receding coaches. Behind us gapes Parson's Tunnel, and next to it the sandstone stack known as the Clerk. School has taught us about Medusa, and even about that other petrefactor, the basilisk, but these are figures of myth, and we cannot imagine how these human ecclesiastics came to be turned to stone. It is safer to look away. Years later, violent storms will wash away the sea wall at this point, and thousands of tons of railway embankment be lost in mudslides, leaving the track hanging, and all stations between Plymouth and Exeter St David's be cut off. But today, we will play on the beach, build castles of sand, select pebbles to take back to the cottage as gifts for our parents, and tomorrow or later, walk along that sea wall, even as far as Teignmouth, trainspotting, and come hurrying back before the light fades, dodging the spray thrown up as the incoming tide crashes against the rocks below.

The mudslides of 2014 that eroded the railway bring me to Ponge himself, a collection of whose prose poems lie before me. Its title poem, *An Unfinished Ode to Mud*, is by no means the longest in the book; that distinction belongs to his seven-and-a-bit page poem *The Pebble* (*Le Galet*), which I have scrupulously avoided reading while engaged in this adventure of memory and imagination. Now that I do, my own efforts seem prosaic by comparison, *'a poor, low, crawling humdrum bitony of trochaics and iambics,'* as George Psalmanazar, a poet I admire almost as much as I admire Francis Ponge, said of Bishop Hare's translation of the Psalms. But here I risk giving my pebble too hard a smack of the hand, so pull back in the nick of time, content with whatever my poem has so far scored, lodging its musings between the lines.

AN INVENTED MAN

Let a man be invented as a poem is,
or as his discourse, of which on a day

void of surprises he imagines himself
both origin and director; let him find

himself drafted, revised, questioned,
challenged and reformed to the least

phrase of his being, which at its best
(its most stubborn, its most articulate)

conforms thought and word in a figure
that, being neither, at once unites both

in the same substance of brain and finger
from which he is himself manipulated;

and let him step sideways from all rhetorics
that elaborate fact to rococo travesties

of what is the case, or the gaudy fabrics
of a conceit that is merely fashionable;

then he will understand he is governed
by the same laws that rule all invention

and since he is fiction, reach after truth
not as transcribers but as conjurors do,

each pass of the hand folding illusion
into illusion so surely that disbelief

surrenders herself to a new act of naming,
and probabilities long since unsuspected,

wake from their sleep in folds of what
may be the case to grow bold and vigorous;

consistent, and so believed; full of grace,
and so giving delight even as they instruct;

artless, as his tongue that pronounced them
valid; and truthful, as they conformed to truth.

BIOGRAPHY

Dan Smith

John Gohorry was born Donald Herbert Fennemore Smith in Coventry in 1943. His parents were Cyril John Smith and Irene Smith (née Ward). His childhood was spent in wartime Coventry with his brother Peter to whom he remained close. From Wyken Colliery School he went on to Bablake School in 1954, and from there to University College London, where he obtained an M.Phil. in 1970.

He taught for thirty-five years in Further and Higher Education, primarily at North Herts College in Hitchin. His retirement in 2006 was followed by a creative explosion, which included publishing twelve books (many with Shoestring Press). This surge was fuelled as much by his working life as by his frequent travel. He spoke French, German and Latin, and his international outlook was reflected by his interests in Eastern philosophy, meditation (becoming vegetarian in the year 2000), Japan, and in walking the Tokaido road. Each is prominent in the bibliography of his work.

John was a father to seven children and step children: Fabian (b1983), Daniel (b1981), Caspar (b1979) who died in infancy, Zoë (b1976), Clare (b1973), Ben (b1971), Gawen (stepchild, b1969), and Melissa (stepchild, b1968). He was also grandfather to sixteen grandchildren. He married his second wife, Gerlinde, in 1981 and they had made plans to celebrate their 40th wedding anniversary in December 2021. John Gohorry died in October 2021 and was buried on 30th November at Wilbury Hills Cemetery in Letchworth Garden City, his home since 1983.

He was a keen runner, chess-player, goalkeeper, gardener, bird-spotter, didgeridoo player and follower of Coventry City Football Cub. His heroes included Samuel Johnson, whose dictionary was one of his prized possessions, and whose portrait he decorated every year to mark his birthday on September 18th. He could often be heard singing, and sometimes rapping. He loved to laugh and joke, explore, take photographs, watch eclipses, ride trains, listen to reggae, eat Turkish delight, visit stone circles, play cards after dinner, and to recover large rocks for subsequent positioning in the garden. He could fix a car with just a lolly stick.

He had an insatiable appetite for theatres, art galleries, concerts and museums. He regularly loaned books from his extensive collection to his children and grandchildren. Alongside the poetry, some of his favourite (and most often recommended) novels were *Zen and the Art of Motorcycle Maintenance*, *Tristram Shandy*, *Moby Dick* and *The Magic Mountain*. Typically, on one occasion he produced a detailed eight-page translation of a key passage in the latter, so that his children could share his enjoyment. A proud family man, he was the most reliable of Chieftains, whose kindness, generosity and good-humour were boundless. He described himself as a paid-up member of the 'every day is a gift' club.

BIBLIOGRAPHY

Books:

A Coventry Crucible by John Gohorry & John Lane (Lapwing Publications, 2021)

Exploring Psalmanazar (Shoestring Press, 2020)

The Stock Exchange of Ideas (Arenig Press, 2019)

Squeak, Budgie! (Smokestack Books, 2019)

Not a Silent Night / Keine Stille Nacht by John Gohorry & Bettine Koch (Shoestring Press, 2017)

Impromptus for George Erdmann & The Good Samaritan, a libretto for a conjectural Abendmusik, 1705 (Lapwing Publications, 2015)

The Age of Saturn (Shoestring Press, 2015)

Adagios on Ré – Adagios en Ré (Lapwing Publications, 2014)

On the Blue Cliff (Dark Age Press, 2012)

Samuel Johnson's Amber (Shoestring Press, 2010)

Forty-Eight Gates (Dark Age Press, 2009)

Imagining Magdeburg (Shoestring Press, 2007)

Talk into the Late Evening (Peterloo Poets, 1992)

A Voyage Round the Moon (Peterloo Poets, 1985)

Pamphlets:

Thirty-Three Ostrich Cadenzas (Shoestring Press, 2017)

Ten Pantomime Sketches (www.johngohorry.co.uk, 2013)

A Manager's Dog (Shoestring Press, 2011)

That Inward Eye with John Lane and William Wordsworth (www.johngohorry.co.uk, 2010)

The Time of Day with John Lane (www.johngohorry.co.uk, 2010)

From the Slopes of Mount Rozan – drawings by Jone Delahaye (www.johngohorry.co.uk, 2009)

Barbarian – mixed media colour image by Jone Delahaye (www.johngohorry.co.uk, 2008)

Stone Places with John Lane – mixed media images by Jone Delahaye (www.johngohorry.co.uk, 2007)

Five Trompe l'Oeil Verses – mixed media images by Jone Delahaye (www.johngohorry.co.uk, 2007)

Barnacle Oak (www.johngohorry.co.uk, 2006)

Eight Chinese Verses – linocut illustrations by Jone Delahaye (in *Take Five 04*, Shoestring Press, 2004)

Imagining Dr Minor – linocut illustrations by Jone Delahaye (Shoestring Press, 2001)

A Life of Merlin – monoprint illustrations by John Gruenwald (Bullnettle Press, San Francisco, 2000)

Arcadian Silver – seven poems (Letchworth, 1998)

Merlin Broadsides – lithograph illustrations by John Gruenwald (Bullnettle Press, San Francisco, 1998)

Ten Oxherding Poems – linocut illustrations by Jone Delahaye (Typographaeum Press, Francestown, New Hampshire, 1997)

Merzbilder – illustrations by Bernd Reichert (Nora Handpresse, Düsseldorf, 1995)

Nocturne in Memory of Freda Downie (Priapus Press, 1994)

Amber – a selection of poems from the prize-winning sequence, Arvon International Poetry Competition 1991 (Arvon Foundation, 1993)

Voices from Lange Halde – woodcut by Werner Brenneke (Nora Handpresse, Düsseldorf, 1990)

A Light for the Birkenkopf – illustrations by George Walker (Wind of Change, Toronto, 1989)

Hobbes's Whale – wood engravings by Simon Brett (Paulinus Press, 1988)

Hinreise nach Sonnehbühl – silk screen illustrations by John Brogden, mixed media illustrations by Werner Brenneke (Nora Handpresse Düsseldorf, 1988)

An Incident in the Plaza del Zocodover, Toledo 1584 – drawings by Peter Lisieski (Bullnettle Press, San Francisco, 1987)

Terra Damnata (Roger Burford Mason, Hitchin, 1987)

A Lecturing Life (Grammelot Press, 1986)

A Letter from Lewis Chaucer to his father, Geoffrey Chaucer (Perdix Press, 1985)

The Coast of Bohemia (Mandeville Press, 1981)

Understudies (Priapus Press, 1980)

A Galanty Show (Fearnhill School Press, 1979)

Norfolk Poems with Roger Burford Mason (Dodman Press, 1978)

Five Poems with a lithograph by Colin Reeve (Kit Cat Press, 1977)

Joining the Dark (Dodman Press, 1975)